Benchmarking Workbook

Benchmarking Workbook
With examples and ready-made forms

Bengt Karlöf

JOHN WILEY & SONS

Chichester · New York · Brisbane · Toronto · Singapore

Original Swedish version published under the title of Arbetsbok i Benchmarking
by Författarna och IHM Förlag AB

Copyright © 1995 by Bengt Karlöf and Svante Östblom

English translation © 1995 by Bengt Karlöf

English translation published 1995 by John Wiley & Sons Ltd,
Baffins Lane, Chichester,
West Sussex PO19 1UD, England

Other Wiley Editorial Offices

John Wiley & Sons, Inc., 605 Third Avenue,
New York, NY 10158-0012, USA

Jacaranda Wiley Ltd, 33 Park Road, Milton,
Queensland 4064, Australia

John Wiley & Sons (Canada) Ltd, 22 Worcester Road,
Rexdale, Ontario M9W 1L1, Canada

John Wiley & Sons (SEA) Pte Ltd, 37 Jalan Pemimpin #05-04,
Block B, Union Industrial Building, Singapore 2057

British Library Cataloguing in Publication Data

A catalogue record for this book is available from the British Library

ISBN 0-471-95587-6

Typeset in 10/12pt Ehrhardt by Dobbie Typesetting Limited
Printed and bound in Great Britain by Bookcraft (Bath) Ltd

Contents

PREFACE   ix

1. INTRODUCTION   1
   Market economy   1
   Internal pricing   1
   Benchmarking   1
      What do others do better?   1
      Efficiency   2
      Process   3

2. WHAT IS BENCHMARKING?   5
   Benchmarking is operative improvement   5
   Phases of benchmarking   5
   Process management and benchmarking   5
      Definition   6
      'Not what, but how' Factors crucial to success   7
      Proof   7
      Influence on culture   7
      New business ideas   7
   Customer focus   8
      What customers value   8
   Internal quality focus   8
      Translating customer demand into production quality   8
   Organization focus   9
      Systems and structures   9
   Cost and productivity focus   9
      Delivering value with minimum input of internal resources   9
   Time and process focus   9
      Critical processes   9
   Internal benchmarking   9
      Inside the company   9
   External benchmarking   10
      Other similar companies   10
   Functional benchmarking   11
      Breakthrough results   11

3. PHASES OF BENCHMARKING   13
    Summary   13

4. BENCHMARKING ORGANIZATION   15
    Plan of action   15

5. WHAT TO BENCHMARK   21
    Start with your own organization   21
      Exploratory phase   21
      The value chain   21
      Essential questions   21
      Make-or-buy analysis   22
      Processes   22
      Primary benchmarking candidates   22
      Relevant area   23
    Identify critical success factors   23
      Hypothesis   23
      Measurements   24
      Set limits!   25

6. BENCHMARKING PARTNERS   31
    Open exchange of information—with whom?   31
    Opt for internal or external benchmarking   31
    Different is not necessarily better   31
    Check comparability   31
    Make contact   32
    Give them what they need to make a decision   32
    Initial meeting   35

7. INFORMATION GATHERING   37
    What information?   37
    Benchmarking is based on trust   37
    Personal meetings   37
    Verify   38
    Balanced score card   38

8. ANALYSIS   49
    Confirm information   49
    Performance gap   49
    Check for comparability   49
    What accounts for differences in performance?   49
    How must practices be changed to achieve better performance? 50

9. **IMPLEMENTATION** 53
   New goals 53
   Information 53
   Implementation plan 53

10. **CASE HISTORIES** 59
    Case 1 59
      Background 59
        Productivity-focused benchmarking—Choice of benchmarking criteria 59
      Aim of benchmarking 60
        Choice of benchmarking partners 60
      Result of analysis 60
        Analysis of production processes and underlying operative content—
        Gap analysis 60
      Benchmarking recommendations and subsequent results 63
    Case 2 63
      Background 63
      Aim of benchmarking 63
        Benchmarking with broad focus on customer-perceived value—
        Choice of benchmarking criteria—Know your own organization—
        Choice of benchmarking partners 66
      Results of the analysis 66
      Benchmarking recommendations and subsequent results 68
    Case 3 68
      Background 68
      Aim of benchmarking 69
        Choice of benchmarking partners—Benchmarking study—
        Information gathering and analysis 69
      Analysis of operative content 70
      Results of benchmarking 72
    Case 4   International benchmarking 74
      Background 74
      Aim of benchmarking 75
        What to benchmark 75
      Comparability 75
      Results of low-resolution exploratory benchmarking 78
      In-depth benchmarking of selected areas 78
        Operation and maintenance 78
      Results of benchmarking 79

11. **FOLLOW-UP AND BENCHLEARNING** 81
    Universal involvement 81
    Skill development as a tool for efficiency 81
      Two routes to efficiency 81
      The third way 82

New routes to efficiency   82
   Efficiency in training   82
Fact-based skill development   83
Benchlearning   83
   On-the-job learning   83
   Foundation   83

12. WORK FORMS   85

Preface

When the book *Benchmarking—A Signpost to Excellence in Quality and Productivity* was published we expected it to be successful, because benchmarking had already proved to have an enormous impact.

The actual result has surpassed our expectations. Benchmarking is advancing at an astonishing rate. The method is *simple, easy to grasp* and *universal*. Anybody can go right ahead and start benchmarking.

We have, however, received numerous enquiries from people asking 'But how do you do it in actual practice?', 'Can you tell us what you did in such and such a case?', and so on.

This Benchmarking Workbook was written to meet an evident need for a 'do-it-yourself' guide to benchmarking. We have included plenty of examples from actual cases as well as a self-diagnostic 'what to do' section for each phase of the process. It also includes forms, checklists and questionnaires to help the novice benchmarker.

The Workbook is intended for use as a basic textbook in our courses on benchmarking, but can also be used separately.

The Workbook was produced in collaboration between the consultants at Karlöf & Partners with special contributions from Agneta Mallander, through her master's dissertation on benchmarking, and our senior partner Bengt Karlöf.

HOW TO USE THE WORKBOOK

Start by reading the theoretical parts (Chapters 1–4) and go on to read through the case studies. Then go back to Chapter 5 and work through the five stages of benchmarking, using the Workbook as a guide. You can do this either as an actual benchmarking project or as an exercise based on the examples in the book.

1

Introduction

MARKET ECONOMY

A market economy is an economic system in which users of goods and services can choose freely among various suppliers. Those suppliers who are not chosen, or chosen too seldom, must either improve their performance or go out of business. Experience shows that this system is highly conducive to efficiency.

In a fully developed market economy, rival companies compete on the same market, and each company can measure its efficiency by the bottom line of its profit–and–loss account. *Parts* of companies, however, deliver to *internal* users. Though the company as a whole operates in a market economy, the internal users cannot choose freely among suppliers. The overall efficiency of the company can be measured, but many of its component functions are never measured at all.

INTERNAL PRICING

Internal pricing systems can be substituted for a market economy, but they are difficult to construct and unfortunately tend to encourage the growth of bureaucracy (negotiations, quotation–writing, invoicing, etc.).

BENCHMARKING

Another way to replace or simulate a market economy is to find reference points (benchmarks) outside the organization itself.

What do others do better?

Benchmarking is a method of improving performance. By comparing your own operations with those of others who perform better in some respects, you can identify possibilities for improvement. The manager who learns how other people do things, and why they get better results, can apply the lessons to his or her own area of responsibility. To be fully effective, benchmarking must be repeated.

BOX 1.1

The Xerox Corporation was one of the first companies to develop and practise benchmarking. When the first Japanese office copiers appeared on the market in 1976, Xerox had dominated the world market for 20 years through its licensing monopoly and had no previous experience of competition. Five years after the Japanese entered the market, Xerox's profits fell to half what they had been the year before. This sparked off a rigorous programme of improvement by Xerox, based on a benchmarking approach.

The idea was to compare the company with others that were getting excellent results, and to learn from them. By measuring its own operations against those of others, Xerox gained insights into ways of developing and initiating action to catch up with its competitors. The ultimate aim was to regain the championship.

Xerox studied the way competitors developed their products, how much they cost to produce, how they were distributed, marketed and sold, how they were invoiced, how supporting activities worked, what the organization looked like and how it operated, and what technology was used. The results came as a shock: Xerox's costs were much higher than those of its competitors.

One study showed that Xerox's *manufacturing cost* in dollars per machine was the same as the *selling price* of Japanese machines! Yet the Japanese were making a profit on that price. Xerox's strategic plan aimed at an annual productivity increase of 8% (compared to the market average of 3%). Benchmarking revealed that it would take an *18%* increase in productivity to catch up with the Japanese in five years. So strategic planning alone would not have been nearly enough to restore profitability.

The product development cycle was another area that proved to have great potential for improvement. Xerox took twice as long as its Japanese competitors to bring a product to market; in addition, it needed five times as many engineers and four times as many design changes, and its design costs were three times as high. Xerox had more than 30 000 faulty units per million compared to less than 1 000 from its competitors.

Efficiency

The efficiency matrix (Figure 1) summarizes the two dimensions of efficiency or businessmanship: productivity and customer-perceived value (utility). Productivity means getting the greatest possible production out of the smallest possible input of some production factor (capital, labour, time, etc.), i.e. maximum output per unit of input. Customer-perceived value means giving customers the greatest possible satisfaction in return for the price they pay. Benchmarking can be used in both of these dimensions, although the 'hard' productivity dimension is easier to measure and therefore more usual.

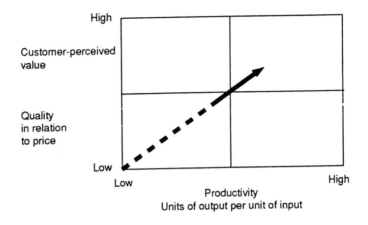

Figure 1.1   Efficiency matrix

Process

In modern business management, the focus of analysis is on operative processes, i.e. on how things are done and how they interact with each other, rather than on formal organizational demarcation lines. Benchmarking concentrates on the central processes of a business.

2
What is benchmarking?

BENCHMARKING IS OPERATIVE IMPROVEMENT

Benchmarking is a method of improving operations. In essence it consists in *looking and learning* from others by comparing yourself with them. Performance and behaviour are not static; they change with time.

Benchmarking is therefore a long-term process. It is a method that involves the whole organization in searching for the best practice outside the company: not just for *what* is done best, but *how* it is done. For an example, see Box 1.1.

PHASES OF BENCHMARKING

Benchmarking, if properly managed, goes through a number of phases. First you decide what needs to be improved, then you choose a candidate for comparison, and finally you measure his or her performance in greater or lesser detail. Benchmarking is most effective if applied continuously.

PROCESS MANAGEMENT AND BENCHMARKING

Process management and benchmarking are closely related concepts. Process management is a matter of regarding a business as the sum of its processes or work flows, which cut across the formal functional organization. By identifying processes (Figure 2.1) you can often discover inefficiencies, e.g. at handover points between departments. In short, it is a matter of 'managing the white spaces in the Table of Organization'.

The first thing to do is to concentrate on customers' needs and to identify and control your processes. This means fine-tuning the organization's work routines. In benchmarking, you compare your own performance with a partner's. The stages of process management, as a rule, are:

(1) *Identify:* Specify and describe processes, and assign an 'owner' to each of them.
(2) *Establish:* Monitor, redesign and improve your processes.
(3) *Develop:* Control and further develop your processes.

These stages fit into the benchmarking method (see Figure 2.2).

Definition

BOX 2.1

Benchmarking rests on two pillars:

(1) *Humility* to recognize that somebody else can do something better than you can.
(2) *Wisdom* to learn the lesson, adapt it to your own situation and take benefit from it.

BOX 2.2

Benchmarking is a process that involves:

(1) Comparing efficiency and processes with good examples and learning the salient features of those processes.
(2) Encouraging willingness to learn, customer-perceived quality and continual improvement.
(3) Helping the organization to identify opportunities for breakthroughs by comparing its processes with good examples.

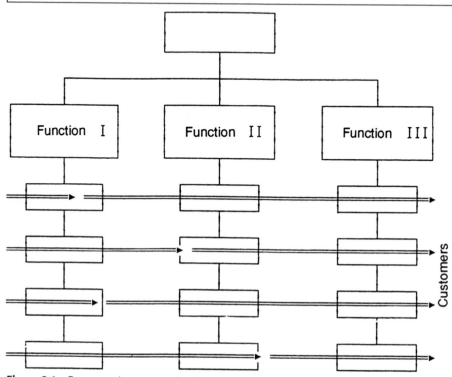

Figure 2.1   Processes in an organization

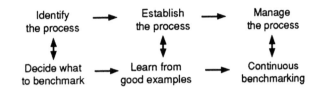

Figure 2.2 Process management and benchmarking

'Not what, but how'
Factors crucial to success

One reason for the growing popularity of benchmarking is that the method penetrates behind finished products and services to the underlying processes. The emphasis is not on *what* other organizations produce, but on *how* they do it. Benchmarking is not a study of quantitative data but a method of discerning underlying operative processes and success factors—how they work and how they differ from your own.

Proof

One advantage of benchmarking is that it allows the managers and employees concerned to see and realize for themselves how much better an activity or process can be run. The whole point of the method is to learn from what others have already accomplished. The proof that others can do and have done better is a powerful incitement to change one's ways.

Influence on culture

Perhaps the greatest long-term advantage of benchmarking is that it moulds a company's corporate culture. The method encourages learning. The repetitive component of benchmarking, and its focus on the performance of the organization, make it highly effective.

New business ideas

Another reason why benchmarking is used by companies like Xerox and IBM is that it has a catalytic effect in generating new business ideas. Seeing how others succeed in getting good results is an inspiration to making improvements that often far surpass one's previous conceptions of what was possible.

CUSTOMER FOCUS

What customers value

Customer-focused benchmarking shows how well your performance matches what customers value and expect, and lets you see how skilled other companies are at satisfying customer demands.

Customer satisfaction and customer relations are good subjects for benchmarking. The following questions can help you get started on benchmarking with that kind of focus:

- How do businesses operate which have aimed for and achieved excellence in their customer relations?
- What do they do to satisfy customers' needs and cement relations?
- How are customer relations measured?
- What systems have been devised to take care of customers who complain?
- What do excellent companies do to stay one jump ahead, and to ascertain how satisfied their customers are?
- How is the market segmented?
- How do customer measurements influence action?

Various market analysis techniques can be used to determine customers' value priorities. Conjoint analysis is one such technique which aims to predict customers' *behaviour* (not just *attitudes*) with regard to price–performance choices. It involves asking people to make choices between hypothetical offerings with systematically varied combinations of attributes. From the answers it is possible to work out how much each individual attribute is worth to customers.

INTERNAL QUALITY FOCUS

Translating customer demand into production quality

Benchmarking with the focus on production quality indicates the required quality level of primary and supporting business activities. Studies with this focus can be based on the following questions:

- How are customers' demands translated into design specifications?
- How many times does an original design have to be modified?
- What systems are used to minimize defects in production?
- What measurements of quality do excellent companies use?

ORGANIZATION FOCUS

Systems and structures

How can you create an organization that will enable the business to deliver top quality in both production and customer satisfaction? Organization-focused benchmarking examines the systems and control methods used, how others develop their personnel, how to inspire enthusiasm for and commitment to the company's goals, and how to use training.

COST AND PRODUCTIVITY FOCUS

Delivering value with minimum input of internal resources

Assuming that you are delivering something that customers value, how can you do it with the lowest possible input of resources? Cost and productivity-focused benchmarking sets out to investigate what levels of cost and productivity can be achieved (i.e. what others have already achieved).

This involves comparing indirect and overhead costs, organizational structure and capacity, the costs of alternative set-ups, what skills are required and how efficiently they can be utilized in a given type of organization. Another suitable subject for a benchmarking study is the company's overall cost structure and the cost drivers in each link of the value chain. Or you can compare the costs of critical processes and what drives them.

TIME AND PROCESS FOCUS

Critical processes

The growing tendency to view a business as the sum of its processes has made time an interesting variable from the standpoint of benchmarking. How long does it take to bring a new product to market, for example, once the management has decided to produce it? The ratio of productive time to total available time is often a highly instructive figure. Inactive and reworking time often exceeds actual value-added time by a wide margin. Non-value-added time can amount to more than 90% of total process time.

INTERNAL BENCHMARKING

Inside the company

Internal benchmarking involves comparisons between different units of the same organization, e.g. regions, branch offices or production facilities.

EXTERNAL BENCHMARKING

Other similar companies

External benchmarking involves looking for benchmarking partners outside your own company. The comparison here is still between identical or similar operations and processes. The benchmarking partner may be a direct competitor, or a company in the same line of business serving a different market in another country. In this case the degree of comparability is high.

BOX 2.3

It is quite common for competitors to collaborate on benchmarking projects in areas where the information shared is not regarded as confidential. Projects of this type are often initiated by trade associations which try to promote exchange of information for the benefit of all their members. One example of this kind of benchmarking co-ordination is the Telecommunications Benchmarking Consortium in America, which consists of a number of companies in direct competition with each other (AT&T, Bell Atlantic, MCI, Ameritech, GTE and others). Its object is to compare, develop and improve primary processes of common interest to all members.

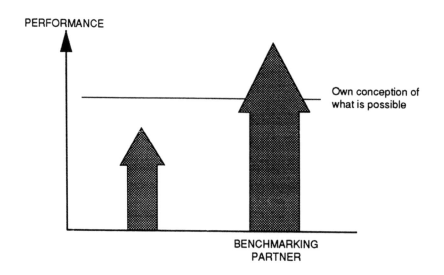

Figure 2.3 Improvement potential of benchmarking

FUNCTIONAL BENCHMARKING

Breakthrough results

Functional benchmarking involves comparisons of products, services, functions or processes with organizations that are worth learning from, no matter what industry they operate in. The results of comparable operations in different industries vary according to how crucial they are to competitiveness in each industry. Customer care, for example, is probably a more critical issue for an international airline than for a local post office. This means that airlines probably have better developed customer care routines which post offices could learn from and imitate.

Functional benchmarking has the potential for making breakthrough-type improvements.

3

Phases of benchmarking

SUMMARY

This summary can be taken to represent what a benchmarking process involves in practice. If you study the scope of the five phases you will realize that benchmarking is not just a conventional comparison of key indicators, but calls for a high degree of commitment on the part of everybody concerned.

(1) Decide what to benchmark:

- Identify the needs of your organization
- Survey your operations
- Identify and study the processes that are critical to results and how they can be measured
- Decide whether detailed benchmarking is required

(2) Identify benchmarking partners:

- Decide whether benchmarking should be internal or external (determine type of case)
- Search for companies worth copying
- Contact potential benchmarking partners to enlist their co-operation
- Pay attention to criticism

(3) Gather information:

- Draw up a questionnaire including definitions and explanations
- Gather information from your own organization
- Gather information from your benchmarking partner and possible other sources
- Check quality of information obtained (confirm and verify to ensure reliability of data)
- Correct for non-comparable factors if any

(4) Analyse:

- Sort and arrange information
- Identify performance gap to best practice and operative factors that explain gap

(5) Implement for effect:

- Secure internal agreement on results of study
- Integrate results with regular business plan
- Prepare a plan for achieving potential improvements indicated by benchmarking
- Redesign processes concerned to make them more efficient
- Introduce redesigned processes

4

Benchmarking organization

The benchmarking process should preferably be run by a team appointed in the initial stage of the project. Members of the team are selected for their skills and motivation. The 'owners' of the studied processes should also be included. It is essential that the organization makes sufficient resources (time, finance and process support) available to support the benchmarking team right from the start. The benchmarking team should be supported by benchmarking specialists, either in-house experts or, for a first-time project, outside consultants. The commissioner of the project should set up a steering committee to which the team leader reports. Active participation by the commissioner is essential to success.

It is further advisable for the steering committee to have access to a suitably composed reference group.

BOX 4.1

All filled-in forms and examples below (ie, filled in or partially filled in forms) refer to a medium-sized development company with profitability problems.

PLAN OF ACTION

A benchmarking project, like any other project, needs to be planned, so we start by drawing up a plan of action (Table 4.1). All project activities should be listed phase by phase (see Chapter 3), stating purpose, person responsible, time and resources required and goal of each activity.

The schedule can also be illustrated by a Gantt chart (Figure 4.2).

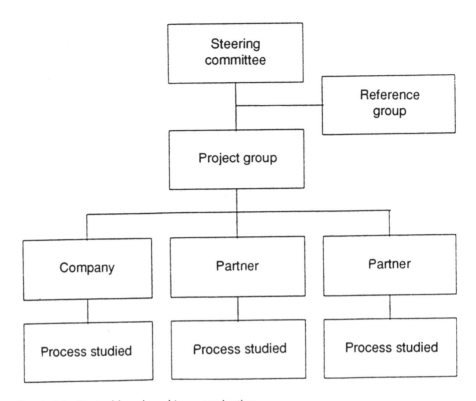

Figure 4.1   Typical benchmarking organization

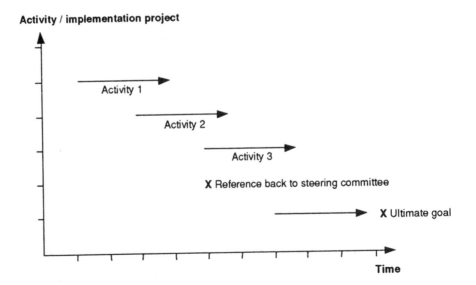

Figure 4.2   Project schedule chart

Table 4.1   Plan of action

Activity	Purpose	Person in charge	Timetable	Goal
Decide what to benchmark	Define task Determine critical parameters for success	Person/ project		
Identify benchmarking partners	Select partner and type of benchmarking	Person/ project		
Report to Steering Committee		Project manager		
Gather information	Benchmarking information	Person/ project		
Analyse	Gap analysis	Person/ project		
Implement	Implement identified improvements	Person/ project		

Table 4.2   Benchmarking planning checklist

Decide what to benchmark	Has our own business been mapped out? Have our own processes been identified? Have the customers and suppliers of these processes been identified? Has the level of detail for benchmarking been decided?
Identify benchmarking partners	Decide upon type of partner Search for partners Identify the partner's main processes Secure acceptance of participation
Gather information	Has the type of information needed been clearly defined? Is information from our organization readily available? Is information available from outside sources? Have we compiled explanatory information? Is the quality of the information controlled? Have we checked the information against our needs? Correct for non-comparable factors
Analyse	Has the information been correctly compiled? Can a gap in performance be observed? Can factors that explain the gap be found?
Implement	Has the result of the benchmarking study been accepted by the organization? Can the results be integrated with our regular business plan? Have alterations of main processes been identified? Have enough resources been allocated to implementation of the changes? Have our skills improved?

Table 4.3   Process survey checklist

Identify	What are our central processes?
	_____
	_____
	_____
	_____
	_____
	What are their goals?
	_____
	_____
	_____
	_____
	_____
	Who owns the processes?
	_____
	_____
	_____
	_____
	_____
	Grouping: primary and support processes
	_____
	_____
	_____
	_____
	_____

Define   Customer needs

_____

_____

_____

_____

_____

Resources

_____

_____

_____

_____

_____

Materials

_____

_____

_____

_____

_____

Analyse   Strengths and weaknesses

_____

_____

_____

_____

_____

5

What to benchmark

START WITH YOUR OWN ORGANIZATION

Exploratory phase

In benchmarking, you should *start with your own organization*. By analysing and understanding customers' needs, and the operative content and *work processes* of your organization, you determine what it is in your organization that needs to be changed. All measures for improvement proceed from the customer. Sometimes suitable subjects for benchmarking are evident, but sometimes you must make a careful analysis of your business to determine the focus of the analysis. Areas and processes that have not previously been studied in detail are often good candidates for benchmarking. Here you can make a division into primary or core processes (the ones that constitute the essence of your business such as taking orders, developing and distributing products, etc.) and support processes (the ones that furnish the primary processes with resources, e.g. administration, recruiting and reporting). See section 'Primary candidates for benchmarking' later in this chapter.

The value chain

It is important that the people involved in a benchmarking project should be familiar with their own organization before the decision on what to benchmark is made. It is a good idea for companies to begin by surveying *their own value chain*. The example in Figure 5.1 refers to the equipment sales and installation branch of Telia, the Swedish national telecom company. Here the value chain is expressed in cost components. If benchmarking is going to focus on costs, it is also advisable to find out what drives the various cost components.

Essential questions

Does input from outside suppliers amount to more than half the cost of the product? If so, the purchasing procedure is a more relevant subject for benchmarking than any of the company's internal functions or processes. How competitive are your suppliers? What sort of relations does your company have with its suppliers? How well do the processes work? Are your suppliers involved in your product development?

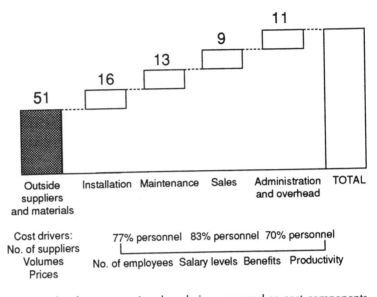

Figure 5.1 Example of a company's value chain, expressed as cost components

Make-or-buy analysis

Another question you should ask yourself is whether you should go on manufacturing or producing everything that you are producing now, or whether there are some things you ought to buy instead in future. Here you weigh the strategic importance of the activity and its contribution to the overall result against the difficulty (or possibility) of finding good external sources of supply. In the matrix in Figure 5.2, the positions of possible outside sources are set in relation to the company's own position.

This example is also taken from the Telia case. The word 'type' in the figure refers to clearly defined organizational units.

Processes

The tendency in benchmarking has been to concentrate more and more on processes. At the beginning of the 1980s Xerox decided, as part of its drive for internal improvement, to view its business as the sum of processes rather than functions. They found that nearly all processes crossed several functional demarcation lines. When the processes were analysed to assess their efficiency it turned out that 80–90% of all malfunctions, bottlenecks, duplication of effort, etc. occurred at the boundary crossing points.

Primary benchmarking candidates

It is usually possible to identify a few processes which between them account for the lion's share of value added in all the company's primary and support activities. Improvement

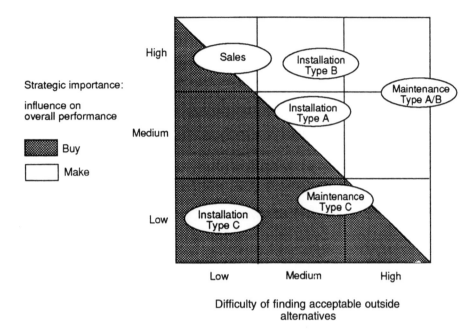

Figure 5.2   Example of a make-or-buy analysis

measures should naturally be concentrated on those areas where they have maximum impact on the organization's performance and results.

By going through the process/function matrix (Table 5.1) you can acquire a picture of your organization's strengths and weaknesses. This makes it easier to identify primary benchmarking candidates. Then, having selected the crucial process, you must describe and analyse it, using the benchmarking process questionnaire (Table 5.2). In the example shown in the matrix, product design and product development appear to be weak and are therefore primary candidates for benchmarking.

After this, use the benchmarking process description (Table 5.3) to develop your thoughts about the selected benchmarking process and how it is quantified (see under 'Measurements' section below).

Relevant area

If the benchmarking team is inexperienced, it is advisable to pick an area which, though relevant to the business, is not the most complex one or the one that represents the organization's most important strategic issue.

IDENTIFY CRITICAL SUCCESS FACTORS

Hypothesis

The job of benchmarking will be easier if the team sets up a hypothesis about the critical

---

BOX 5.1

Xerox's ten questions

(1) What is the most critical factor for success in my function/organization (e.g. satisfied customers, cost/revenue index, return on investment)?
(2) What factors cause most problems (failure to perform as expected)?
(3) What products or services reach external customers?
(4) What factors make customers satisfied?
(5) What specific (operative) problems have been identified in the organization?
(6) Where is pressure of competition felt in the organization?
(7) What are the greatest costs (or cost drivers) in the organization?
(8) Which functions account for the largest share of costs?
(9) Which functions offer the greatest opportunities for improvement?
(10) Which functions offer the greatest opportunities (or potential) for differentiating the organization from its competitors in the market-place?

---

success factors (benchmarking criteria) that the project is supposed to identify. This hypothesis will help to keep the discussion and data gathering structured and relevant. The hypothesis may be based on a review of previously published material (see Box 5.2).

Measurements

It may also be advisable at an early stage in the proceedings to think about what *units of measurement* may be available for use, even if they may not actually describe the best demonstrated practice. It may turn out that what you hoped to measure no longer exists

---

BOX 5.2

The search for a hypothesis concerning critical performance factors may for example show that three factors, more than any others, contribute to Volvo's aggregate performance in the area of product development. Those three factors are *individual engineering skills*, *project management* and *systems* for solution of production problems at an early stage in the development process. A benchmarking team that visits Volvo will probably have neither the time nor the opportunity (access) to form an overall appreciation of Volvo's product development capability, but it can ask specific questions relevant to what it is most interested in, such as the average age of project engineers, the number of projects the average engineer has previously worked on, and the number of drawings that have been altered after having been initially approved.

---

in those businesses that have advanced furthest in the area you are studying. That in itself is a valuable insight.

The benchmarking process description sheet (Table 5.3) gives some indication of what kind of measurements are essential and relevant to the process. Use the determination of benchmarking criteria sheet (Table 5.4) to analyse your proposed benchmarking criterion.

Set limits!

One of the commonest mistakes that companies make is failing to set hard limits for a benchmarking project, but instead trying to collect as much information as possible from all sorts of places and visiting as many companies as possible. This leaves no time over for analysis. One way to avoid this trap, for example, is to make an early short list of which activities/processes are candidates for benchmarking, with priorities based on economic importance, future strategic importance, make-or-buy considerations and internal willingness to change[1] (Figure 5.3).

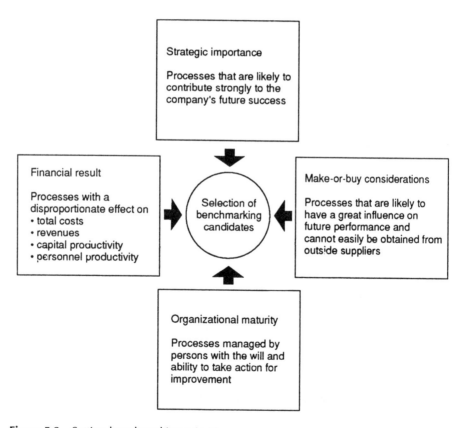

Figure 5.3   Setting benchmarking priorities

---

[1]Walleck, O'Halloran, Leader, McKinsey Quarterly, No 1, 1991

Table 5.1 Business process/function matrix

Main processes and subprocesses	Functions					
	Sales	Production	Development	Marketing	Finance	Logistics
Customer orders						
Customer relations	▪ (Average)				▪ (Strong)	
Pricing		▪ (Strong)				
Production						
Distribution						
Packing				▪ (Weak)		
Purchasing						
Supplier relations						
Development						
Prototypes						
Market research						
After market						
Customer complaints						
Field service						
Guarantees						
Business control						
Budgeting						
Financing						
Recruitment						
Personnel development						
Strategic planning						

Evaluation of strength: ▪ Strong ▪ Average ▪ Weak

Table 5.2   Benchmarking process questionnaire

(1)   Describe the process, its purpose, its objectives and the functions involved, with
special emphasis on cross-overs between functions.

_____

_____

_____

_____

_____

(2)   How does this process influence the company's goals and its earnings?

_____

_____

_____

_____

(3)   How can this process be measured in terms of cost, quality and time? How would you
define a high standard in these terms? How can improvements be measured?

_____

_____

_____

_____

(4)   What categories of personnel are involved in this process, and what types of skills are
needed?

_____

_____

_____

_____

(5)   The process does not perform as it should, or costs too much. Has it ever been
reconstructed before, and if so how?

_____

_____

_____

_____

(6)   What conceivable benchmarking partners exist?

_____

_____

_____

_____

Table 5.3 Benchmarking process description

Description of process (diagram)			
Function(s) to which process belongs and handovers between separate functions			
Objectives of process			
Customers for process			
Suppliers to process			
Targets for process performance			
	Present level	Trend	Target
Costs			
Time			
Quality measurements			

Table 5.4 Determination of benchmarking criteria (BC)

Benchmarked process(es)
Proposed measurements
Reason for choice of measurements
'Owner' of process

Key questions
(1) Do the BC give a thorough and relevant description of the process?
(2) The number of BC used should be kept as small as possible. Can certain criteria be omitted?
(3) Can relevant data be obtained?
(4) What data are quantifiable/not quantifiable?
(5) Can the BC be measured over a period of time?
(6) Are the BC recognized internally/externally?
(7) Does an improvement in the BC mean that the whole process is improved?
(8) How would a radical improvement in the BC affect the company's net income?

Table 5.5   Questions

(1)   Go through Xerox's ten questions (Box 5.1) for your business.

_____

_____

_____

(2)   What processes are weak in your business?
      (Use the business process/function matrix sheet (Table 5.1).)

_____

_____

_____

(3)   Go through the benchmarking process questionnaire (Table 5.2) for two or three weak processes.
      Choose the most relevant one.
      Which one did you pick, and why?

_____

_____

_____

(4)   What would be a suitable benchmarking criterion?
      Can it be measured?
      (Use the determination of benchmarking criteria sheet (Table 5.4).)

_____

_____

_____

(5)   Try to draw an activity chart. How can the process be described? (Use the benchmarking process
      description sheet (Table 5.3).)

_____

_____

_____

6

Benchmarking partners

OPEN EXCHANGE OF INFORMATION—WITH WHOM?

When you have decided *what* to benchmark, it is time to think about with whom you are going to do it. The object of this second phase of benchmarking is to identify and establish relations with organizations which represent good examples of what you want to benchmark. The term 'benchmarking partner' indicates that the relationship you want is one in which information is freely exchanged. It is often better to get closely acquainted with a couple of organizations whose results are clearly better than yours than to make a superficial study of a large number.

Use the business comparison: key indicator analysis sheet (Table 6.1) to make a first rough short list of interesting objects of comparison.

OPT FOR INTERNAL OR EXTERNAL BENCHMARKING

The first question is whether to go for internal or external benchmarking. This depends on whether your operations can be substantially improved by an internal comparison, e.g. with other regions or companies in the same group. Otherwise you will have to look elsewhere. Naturally, the better you already are, the harder it will be to find somebody who is better than you (see Figure 6.1).

DIFFERENT IS NOT NECESSARILY BETTER

Companies that regularly use benchmarking often take the line that the companies they compare themselves with do not have to be the very best in the world. As long as their performance is distinctly better than the home company's, they are probably worth studying. Some caution is called for in comparing yourself with others; do not assume that anything done differently from the way you do it is necessarily done better.

CHECK COMPARABILITY

In manufacturing processes, comparability of product characteristics (size of product, volume of production, variety of components and materials, etc.) is a critical aspect. In service processes, the critical factors for comparability may be number of services performed daily, spare part requirements or the customer-perceived value of repairs.

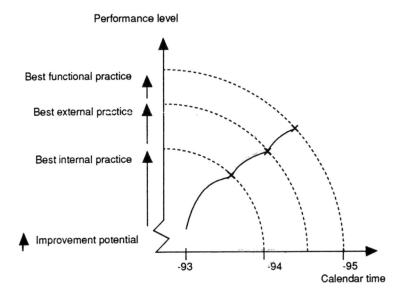

Figure 6.1 The level from which you start determines where to look for methods that can improve your performance

A simple key indicator analysis (Table 6.1) can be a useful aid to finding suitable benchmarking partners.

MAKE CONTACT

When you have found benchmarking partners, it is time to approach them. The first contact with a prospective partner has one purpose only: to establish contact and fix a time for a personal presentation. There is seldom any difficulty about obtaining agreement to a meeting with no strings attached.

GIVE THEM WHAT THEY NEED TO MAKE A DECISION

The initial meeting has two purposes: firstly to *explain the nature of the project*, and secondly to *furnish potential participants with the information they need* to make a decision. The advantage of gaining low-cost access to new knowledge and learning about other businesses should be emphasized. Although the prospective partners have been chosen because they represent excellence in some respect (which they are often flattered to hear), in nearly every case *all* the parties involved acquire new and useful knowledge.

Having identified your partner, you should 'map' them to acquire a quick outline picture, using the benchmarking partner analysis sheet (Table 6.2).

Table 6.1   Business comparison: key indicator analysis

Indicators	Company		
	X	Y	Z
Return on equity after tax income %			
Return on working capital before tax %			
Solidity			
Capital turnover rate			
Inventory			
Balance sheet total			
Sales per employee $			
R&D costs % of sales			
Return on investments			
Net financial result % of sales			
Warranty costs %			
Market share %			
Goods returned % of deliveries			

Table 6.2   Benchmarking partner analysis

Characteristics		Companies		
Size	Sales			
	No. of employees			
Ownership	Public companies: 5 largest shareholders			
	Closely held companies: families			
Business concept/mission				
Main products				
Organization	Functional			
	Divisionalized			
	Matrix			
	Other			
Cultural factors	Formalism			
	Group control			
	Openness			
Specific business skills				
Strategy				

Table 6.3 Questions

(1)	What good (or excellent) examples of partners for the chosen process are available? Is a functional approach feasible?
(2)	What are our own key indicators? Are we prepared to disclose them?
(3)	How will the project be organized? Draw up a timetable and activity chart, sketch in organization and manning.
(4)	What preparations do we need to make for the initial meeting?

INITIAL MEETING

At the initial meeting you should describe:

- your business
- the purpose and goals of the project
- the type of information required
- the degree of detail desired
- measures of performance to be used
- a timetable for the project
- information to be reported back to partners

Provided that the proposed partners agree to participate, you can proceed to the data-gathering and analysis phases. If they do not agree, their decision must of course be respected.

7

Information gathering

WHAT INFORMATION?

When you have decided how you are going to benchmark, you must also decide what kind of information will be needed, if you have not already done so. A process survey checklist (see Table 4.3) is useful here. A couple of fully comparable units of measurement are worth far more than masses of unverified and only partly comprehensible information. Draw up a data acquisition form to specify the information you want, and define the terms you use. Figure 7.1 shows some examples (reproduced full size at the end of the Workbook) of the kinds of forms that could be used. Sometimes a form will need to be accompanied by a list of definitions.

Information gathering often starts at a coarse level and proceeds from there to detailed analysis of factors like personnel, time and sales efficiency.

The starting-point for data acquisition is your own business. Information gathering begins at home:

- The benchmarking team must *familiarize itself with its own organization.*
- The benchmarking team must test the data-gathering model that is to be used.
- This procedure gives the benchmarking process a firm foundation.

BENCHMARKING IS BASED ON TRUST

Information can be obtained from chosen benchmarking partners via publications, questionnaires, telephone interviews, etc. Unlike competition analysis, which often uses a great number of sources to acquire confidential information, *benchmarking relies on mutual exchange of information.* It is therefore very important to define what kind of information is being sought.

PERSONAL MEETINGS

The most fruitful, and recommended, method of gathering information is by personal visits and interviews. Yet one of the commonest planning errors in benchmarking is to underestimate the time required for getting information from other companies.

Information from other companies must *always* be treated as confidential unless otherwise agreed.

VERIFY

The data you acquire must always be verified.

BALANCED SCORE CARD

Successful use of benchmarking makes strict demands on the quality of your reporting system. One way to make a balanced presentation of a small number of critical economic and operative indicators is called the 'balanced score card' method. With this system it is possible to measure operations from, say, four angles: internal, development, improvement and conventional economics.

(1)   What do customers think of the organization's performance?
(2)   What must the organization be good at and get steadily better at?
(3)   Can the organization continue to develop and improve?
(4)   How attractive is the organization to its owners?

Region . . . .   Shop . . . .

	Product	Services	Miscellaneous	Total
Sales External	[_____]	[_____]	[_____]	[_____]
Internal	[_____]	[_____]	[_____]	[_____]
Commissions	[_____]	[_____]	[_____]	[_____]
Margin contribution 1	[_____]	[_____]	[_____]	[_____]
Margin contribution 1%	[_____]	[_____]	[_____]	[_____]
Price reductions %	[_____]	[_____]	[_____]	[_____]
Wastage %	[_____]	[_____]	[_____]	[_____]
Discounts %	[_____]	[_____]	[_____]	[_____]
Direct costs:				
Personnel	[_____]	[_____]	[_____]	[_____]
Premises, total	[_____]	[_____]	[_____]	[_____]
Marketing, national	[_____]	[_____]	[_____]	[_____]
Marketing, local	[_____]	[_____]	[_____]	[_____]
Computer system	[_____]	[_____]	[_____]	[_____]
Training	[_____]	[_____]	[_____]	[_____]
Miscellaneous	[_____]	[_____]	[_____]	[_____]
Depreciation	[_____]	[_____]	[_____]	[_____]
Indirect costs:				
Region	[_____]	[_____]	[_____]	[_____]
Retail organization	[_____]	[_____]	[_____]	[_____]
Inventory booked 31/12	[_____]	[_____]	[_____]	[_____]
Shop area, m^2	[_____]	[_____]	[_____]	[_____]
of which sales area, m^2	[_____]	[_____]	[_____]	[_____]
Employees:				
on 1 Jan 1994	[_____]	[_____]	[_____]	[_____]
on 31 Dec 1994	[_____]	[_____]	[_____]	[_____]
Average for year	[_____]	[_____]	[_____]	[_____]

Directly connected to Head Office   [___] Yes   [___] No

Catchment area (population)   [_____]

Location: [_____]

(Well or badly situated urban, shopping centre, rural)

Figure 7.1 (part one)   Benchmarking: shop questionnaire (1994 results)

Date

Manager

List all employees, including those not at work (maternity leave, long illness, etc.)

Region

Shop

Name	Age	Education	Employed by company	Union member	Shop experience elsewhere Where?	Years	Time in shop	Salary

Figure 7.1 (part two) Benchmarking: personnel analysis

					Total	Remarks
MARKET	**Market**	....	....	....	....	
	Market analysis	....	....	....	....	
	Market planning	....	....	....	....	
	Other (. . . . .)	....	....	....	....	
	Advertising					
	Marketing communications	....	....	....	....	
	Artwork	....	....	....	....	
	Sales promotion	....	....	....	....	
	Point-of-sale material	....	....	....	....	
	Other (. . . . .)	....	....	....	....	
PRODUCT	**Product specification**	....	....	....	....	
	Product knowledge	....	....	....	....	
	Product range composition	....	....	....	....	
	Product range strategy	....	....	....	....	
	Sales planning	....	....	....	....	
	Other (. . . . .)	....	....	....	....	
PRODUCT DEVELOPMENT	**Product development**	....	....	....	....	
	Idea	....	....	....	....	
	Specification	....	....	....	....	
	Development	....	....	....	....	
	Testing	....	....	....	....	
	Documentation	....	....	....	....	
	Other (. . . . .)	....	....	....	....	
PURCHASING	**Purchasing**	....	....	....	....	
	Contact with suppliers	....	....	....	....	
	Cost negotiations	....	....	....	....	
	Other (. . . . .)	....	....	....	....	
	Ordering	....	....	....	....	
	Piecemeal buying	....	....	....	....	
	Other (. . . . .)	....	....	....	....	
LOGISTICS	**Dispatching**	....	....	....	....	
	Shipping	....	....	....	....	
	Other (. . . . .)	....	....	....	....	
	Stocks	....	....	....	....	
	Storeroom work	....	....	....	....	
	Picking	....	....	....	....	
	Reception	....	....	....	....	
	Stocktaking	....	....	....	....	
	Data input	....	....	....	....	
	Other (. . . . .)	....	....	....	....	
ADMINISTRATION	**Personnel**	....	....	....	....	
	Salaries and wages	....	....	....	....	
	Union agreements	....	....	....	....	
	Consultation	....	....	....	....	
	Training	....	....	....	....	
	Other (. . . . .)	....	....	....	....	
	Accounting	....	....	....	....	
	Ledger	....	....	....	....	
	Customer and supplier accounts	....	....	....	....	
	Invoicing	....	....	....	....	
	Payments	....	....	....	....	
	Budgeting	....	....	....	....	
	Costing	....	....	....	....	
	Other (. . . . .)	....	....	....	....	

Figure 7.1 (part three) Benchmarking: personnel analysis (*continues overleaf*)

					Total	Remarks

ADMINISTRATION	**Quality**	. . . .	. . . .	. . . .	. . . .	
(continued)	Follow-up of ISO 9000	. . . .	. . . .	. . . .	. . . .	
	Standardization	. . . .	. . . .	. . . .	. . . .	
	Other (. . . . .)	. . . .	. . . .	. . . .	. . . .	
	Internal service	. . . .	. . . .	. . . .	. . . .	
	Building	. . . .	. . . .	. . . .	. . . .	
	Office	. . . .	. . . .	. . . .	. . . .	
	Cleaning	. . . .	. . . .	. . . .	. . . .	
	Delivery	. . . .	. . . .	. . . .	. . . .	
	PABX	. . . .	. . . .	. . . .	. . . .	
	Other (. . . . .)	. . . .	. . . .	. . . .	. . . .	
	Secretarial	. . . .	. . . .	. . . .	. . . .	
	Typing	. . . .	. . . .	. . . .	. . . .	
	Bookings	. . . .	. . . .	. . . .	. . . .	
	Other (. . . . .)	. . . .	. . . .	. . . .	. . . .	
SALES	**Cash register**	. . . .	. . . .	. . . .	. . . .	
	Behind counter in shop	. . . .	. . . .	. . . .	. . . .	
	Other (. . . . .)	. . . .	. . . .	. . . .	. . . .	
	Customer contact	. . . .	. . . .	. . . .	. . . .	
	Telephone	. . . .	. . . .	. . . .	. . . .	
	In shop	. . . .	. . . .	. . . .	. . . .	
	Sale of services	. . . .	. . . .	. . . .	. . . .	
	Sale of products	. . . .	. . . .	. . . .	. . . .	
	Other sales	. . . .	. . . .	. . . .	. . . .	
	Enquiries	. . . .	. . . .	. . . .	. . . .	
	Other (. . . . .)	. . . .	. . . .	. . . .	. . . .	
	Other sales work	. . . .	. . . .	. . . .	. . . .	
	Outdoor selling	. . . .	. . . .	. . . .	. . . .	
	Other (. . . . .)	. . . .	. . . .	. . . .	. . . .	
MANAGEMENT	**Management**	. . . .	. . . .	. . . .	. . . .	
	Costing	. . . .	. . . .	. . . .	. . . .	
	Monitoring and control	. . . .	. . . .	. . . .	. . . .	
	Other (. . . . .)	. . . .	. . . .	. . . .	. . . .	
AFTER-MARKET	**Servicing**	. . . .	. . . .	. . . .	. . . .	
	Repairs	. . . .	. . . .	. . . .	. . . .	
	Maintenance	. . . .	. . . .	. . . .	. . . .	
	Other (. . . . .)	. . . .	. . . .	. . . .	. . . .	
DATA	**EDP system**	. . . .	. . . .	. . . .	. . . .	
PROCESSING	Development	. . . .	. . . .	. . . .	. . . .	
	Salaries and wages	. . . .	. . . .	. . . .	. . . .	
	Sales	. . . .	. . . .	. . . .	. . . .	
	Logistics	. . . .	. . . .	. . . .	. . . .	
	Operations	. . . .	. . . .	. . . .	. . . .	
	Miscellaneous	. . . .	. . . .	. . . .	. . . .	
	Other (. . . . .)	. . . .	. . . .	. . . .	. . . .	

Make a separate list here of services bought in from region or elsewhere:

. . . .	. . . .	. . . .	. . . .	
. . . .	. . . .	. . . .	. . . .	
. . . .	. . . .	. . . .	. . . .	
. . . .	. . . .	. . . .	. . . .	
. . . .	. . . .	. . . .	. . . .	
. . . .	. . . .	. . . .	. . . .	
. . . .	. . . .	. . . .	. . . .	
. . . .	. . . .	. . . .	. . . .	

Figure 7.1 (part four)

Monday

Region. . . . . Shop. . . . . Week no. . . . . .

Time	Callers entering shop	Callers in shop known	Callers in shop unknown	Number of staff at work	Total transactions/receipts
8–9					
9–10					
10–11					
11–12					
12–13					
13–14					
14–15					
15–16					
16–17					
17–18					
18–19					

Sales
Product. . . . .
Total. . . . .
of which cash. . . . .
of which invoiced. . . . .

Tuesday

Region. . . . . Shop. . . . . Week no. . . . . .

Time	Callers entering shop	Callers in shop known	Callers in shop unknown	Number of staff at work	Total transactions/receipts
8–9					
9–10					
10–11					
11–12					
12–13					
13–14					
14–15					
15–16					
16–17					
17–18					
18–19					

Sales
Product. . . . .
Total. . . . .
of which cash. . . . .
of which invoiced. . . . .

Wednesday

Region. . . . . Shop. . . . . Week no. . . . . .

Time	Callers entering shop	Callers in shop known	Callers in shop unknown	Number of staff at work	Total transactions/receipts
8–9					
9–10					
10–11					
11–12					
12–13					
13–14					
14–15					
15–16					
16–17					
17–18					
18–19					

Sales
Product. . . . .
Total. . . . .
of which cash. . . . .
of which invoiced. . . . .

Thursday

Region. . . . . Shop. . . . . Week no. . . . . .

Time	Callers entering shop	Callers in shop known	Callers in shop unknown	Number of staff at work	Total transactions/receipts
8–9					
9–10					
10–11					
11–12					
12–13					
13–14					
14–15					
15–16					
16–17					
17–18					
18–19					

Sales
Product. . . . .
Total. . . . .
of which cash. . . . .
of which invoiced. . . . .

Friday

Region. . . . . Shop. . . . . Week no. . . . . .

Time	Callers entering shop	Callers in shop known	Callers in shop unknown	Number of staff at work	Total transactions/receipts
8–9					
9–10					
10–11					
11–12					
12–13					
13–14					
14–15					
15–16					
16–17					
17–18					
18–19					

Sales
Product. . . . .
Total. . . . .
of which cash. . . . .
of which invoiced. . . . .

Saturday

Region. . . . . Shop. . . . . Week no. . . . . .

Time	Callers entering shop	Callers in shop known	Callers in shop unknown	Number of staff at work	Total transactions/receipts
8–9					
9–10					
10–11					
11–12					
12–13					
13–14					
14–15					
15–16					
16–17					
17–18					
18–19					

Sales
Product. . . . .
Total. . . . .
of which cash. . . . .
of which invoiced. . . . .

Figure 7.1 (part five)

Product group: . . . .

Customer category: Internal . . . .   External . . . .

Selection criteria	Supplier How do we think the customer will rate utility factors?					Supplier How do we rate importance?					Customer What is the contractor's delivery capability?				
	Most important				Not important	Most important				Not important	Good				Bad
	5	4	3	2	1	5	4	3	2	1	5	4	3	2	1
Low price															
Delivery on schedule															
Accessible for enquiries															
Takes full responsibility															
Uses new technology															
High technical quality and competence															
Uses proven technology															
Easy to buy from															
Understands what customers want															
Flexible and quick															
Known contact person															
Provides customer training															
Takes account of future requirements															
Courteous and helpful															
Specified invoices															
Gives guarantees															
ISO 9000 certified															
Right first time															
Can give references															
Environment conscious															

Figure 7.1 (part six)   Determination of customer-perceived value

| Salesperson | | Week no. | |

| District | Customers | | Number |

Number of	Cold calls	Telephone	_____	Number
		Personal	_____	Number
	Meetings	New customers	_____	Number
		Old customers	_____	Number
	Quotations		_____	Number
	Contacts	New customers	_____	Number
		Old customers	_____	Number

Customers per sales step	Suspects	_____	Number
	Prospects	_____	Number
	Ordering	_____	Number

Orders	Average order	Products	_____	£
		Accessories	_____	£
		Service agreement	_____	£
		Total	_____	£
	Number			Number
	Sales to New customers	_____	£

Figure 7.1 (part seven)   Data acquisition form—sales efficiency

Use of time	Cold calls	Telephone	————————	Hours
		Personal	————————	Hours
	Meetings	New customers	————————	Hours
		Old customers	————————	Hours
	Contacts	New customers	————————	Hours
		Old customers	————————	Hours
	Administration	Engineering	————————	Hours
		Quotations	————————	Hours
		Orders	————————	Hours
		Miscellaneous	————————	Hours
	Education	External	————————	Hours
		Internal	————————	Hours
	Training	External	————————	Hours
		Internal	————————	Hours
	Travel		————————	Hours
	Support of other functions	Service	————————	Hours
		Delivery	————————	Hours
	Other		————————	Hours

Company	Contact	Meeting

Figure 7.1 (part eight) Data acquisition forms

Table 7.1 Questions

(1)	What information is needed about the chosen process?

_____

_____

_____

_____

| (2) | How can we make sure that the information is clear and consistent? |

_____

_____

_____

_____

| (3) | How do we design a data acquisition form for the present case? |

_____

_____

_____

_____

| (4) | What are our own data? |

_____

_____

_____

_____

| (5) | What central definitions need to be developed? |

_____

_____

_____

_____

8
Analysis

CONFIRM INFORMATION

Before analysis starts, it must be confirmed that all the information received is correct.

PERFORMANCE GAP

Information received is compiled and various measures of comparison applied to identify differences (performance gaps) between companies (Figure 8.1). Purely numerical information should be treated with caution until the underlying operative content and work processes have been investigated and understood.

CHECK FOR COMPARABILITY

It is important to check whether any non-comparable factors exist, i.e. circumstances and influences that make the comparison 'unfair'. There may, for example, be differences in operative content, scope of operations (e.g. service commitments and inclusion or exclusion of materials consumed), market conditions (e.g. number of customers served), and cost situation (e.g. urban or rural area).

WHAT ACCOUNTS FOR DIFFERENCES IN PERFORMANCE?

The measurements used in the comparison, carefully checked and purged of non-comparable factors, can be compiled to show the gap in perfomance between the companies compared. The knowledge and facts produced by information gathering are used to analyse and appreciate *why* performance differs. The companies use different processes; process mapping, together with the measurements, gives a clue to the difference in performance.

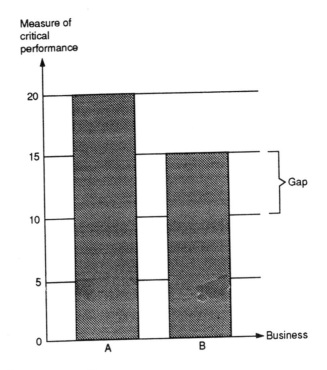

Figure 8.1   Gap measurement

HOW MUST PRACTICES BE CHANGED
TO ACHIEVE BETTER PERFORMANCE?

The collected information, analyses and conclusions are documented in a benchmarking report. This report provides input for the real purpose of the study: to *change practices* in order to achieve the identified best performance. The findings of the study may result in some parts of the business being called in question: should they still be handled in-house, or farmed out to outside suppliers?

The benchmarking: new goals sheet (Table 8.1) summarizes the figures and goal description resulting from the benchmarking exercise.

Table 8.1   Benchmarking: new goals

Critical success parameters	Measures of performance			Partner
Process	Present level	Short-term goal Year	Long-term goal Year	Company: Date:

Changes needed to attain goals
Short-term:
Long-term:

Table 8.2   Questions

(1)   What goals must be attained to achieve radically better results?
Has the benchmarking partner attained them?

_____

_____

_____

_____

(2)   What subprocesses merit further study?

_____

_____

_____

_____

(3)   What non-comparable factors must be adjusted in order to
evaluate performance?

_____

_____

_____

_____

(4)   Are there variables that explain the existence of the gaps found?

_____

_____

_____

_____

9
Implementation

NEW GOALS

Formulate the results of the benchmarking study as new goals for the business, and draw up a plan for implementation.

The benchmarking implementation plan sheet (Table 9.1) is used to describe the goals briefly and state the desired results of the changes.

INFORMATION

Union representatives are an interested party who should always be informed of the results. Benchmarking provides knowledge and decision input for making necessary changes. Especially in cases where the conclusions are bad news for personnel (e.g. overmanning), benchmarking provides the evidence to convince the people concerned of the necessity.

IMPLEMENTATION PLAN

Having drawn up the implementation plan, put it into effect. There are seven factors that determine successful implementation:

(1) *All heads of profit centres must take part:* Nobody can be allowed to opt out of the process of change. Other non-managerial employees should also be involved as far as possible.
(2) *Successful implementation demands commitment:* Benchmarking has the ability to arouse enthusiasm for improvement.
(3) *Goals and strategies must be understood:* Overriding goals and strategies must be broken down into parts and *communicated*.
(4) *There must be a clear schedule for action:* A plan of action is needed to tell everybody how changes are to be made and what they will accomplish. The main function of the timetable is to keep up the pace. Those responsible can check how much progress they have made (see below).
(5) *The management must give the project priority:* Success is conditional on management participation in the process of change.

(6) *Information:* The project leader has a duty to *provide* information; the organization has a duty to *seek* information.

(7) *Energy and perseverance:* These are essential to success in making changes.

Implementation can also take the form of a project (see project description, Table 9.2).

When the recommendations of the benchmarking analysis have been implemented, the five-stage benchmarking process is complete.

Table 9.1 Benchmarking implementation plan

	Company			
	Own company	Partner X	Partner Y	Partner Z
Benchmarked process:				
Process owner:				
Measures of performance:				
Goals				
Short-term:				
Long-term:				
Describe desired result:				

Table 9.2 Project description

Name of project:
Person in charge:
Members of project group:

Purpose of project:

Description of project:

Requirements for implementation/investments:

Consequences:

Timetable/allocation of responsibilities:

Table 9.3   Questions

(1)   List probable implementation projects.
      Will investment be required?

      _____

      _____

      _____

      _____

(2)   What restrictions must we take into account?

      _____

      _____

      _____

      _____

(3)   Can we count on the seven factors for success in implementation?
      How can we make sure?

      _____

      _____

      _____

      _____

10

Case histories

CASE 1

Background

This concerns productivity benchmarking in a contracting business. The case illustrates the common benchmarking issue of productivity in work processes.

Company E does both contracting (installation) and maintenance work. E operates in a metropolitan area and has five departments, four of them engaged in contracting. E has an annual turnover of about £90 million and *sells its services internally at cost price*. There is thus no profit figure by which to measure E's efficiency.

The corporate culture puts heavy emphasis on quality. Both workmanship and service level are of a very high standard. However, the company is not specially cost-conscious. Indeed, it has no incentive to be cost-conscious, since the users of its services are not free to buy from other suppliers.

Productivity-focused benchmarking

E had been trying for several years to reduce its costs and rationalize its operations. However, the management had noted indications that productivity was still not good enough. Increasing competition on the market will eventually make it impossible to maintain higher production costs than other suppliers. Production cost is one of the most critical success factors for E, so the benchmarking study inevitably had to focus on cost. To catalyse a process of change, the management decided to call in a firm of consultants.

Pressure of competition is hardest on the contracting side. The management therefore wished to limit the benchmarking exercise to contracting operations only. Competition had forced them to take extensive action to boost productivity, and to cut their prices. The management of E wanted to know how their own contracting operations compared price-wise with the open market and to acquire experience from organizations operating under market pressure, especially since there already were other companies in the market capable of taking over some parts of E's contracting business.

Choice of benchmarking criteria

Productivity was measured within the company chiefly by calculating total production cost per chargeable hour. The departments also monitored chargeability (the proportion of hours worked that were actually billed). The comparison was based on production cost per hour because this was a traditional in-house yardstick. It is easier to accept new performance goals if they are expressed in familiar terms.

Aim of benchmarking

Choice of benchmarking partners

E had never operated on the open market. By getting tenders from outside subcontractors and trying to calculate backwards to their prices, the management had acquired some notion of prevailing cost levels. An external study would provide more useful information than an internal one. They therefore wanted to find a couple of other companies engaged in the same type of business and find out what their cost levels were and how they had achieved them. The primary aim was not to find the absolute productivity champions, but rather partners whose operations their own organization could identify with. Since E was sheltered from competition, it was bound to find plenty of potential for improvement anyway.

Result of analysis

The comparison between the partners referred exclusively to the cost of producing an hour's worth of chargeable work. The billed price must cover material and labour costs. Cost of materials is an important aspect on the open market, but since E has its own central material supply department, and is thus unable to influence material prices, the comparison concentrated on labour costs. In this case materials were an invariant, non-comparable factor.

Analysis of production processes and underlying operative content

Production cost was defined and set against the number of chargeable hours worked in the first half of the year (Figure 10.1). A chargeable hour is defined as an hour booked as productive working time. Using chargeable hours as the unit has the advantage of high comparability, because they are defined the same way by all the units concerned.

Gap analysis

E's cost disadvantage in the categories of travel, expenses and training, i.e. the bulk of miscellaneous personnel costs, was as much as 96%. The reason was that the partner company's training costs are paid for by its material and equipment suppliers, and that

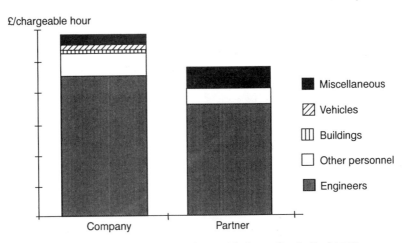

Figure 10.1   Total production cost per chargeable hour, first half of 1992

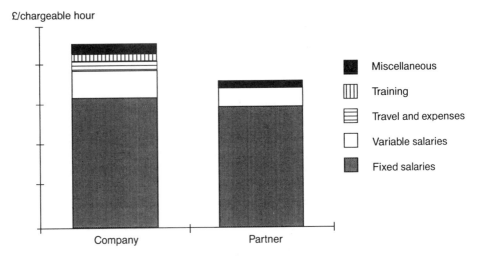

Figure 10.2   Personnel cost per chargeable hour for field engineers

it does not as a rule pay expenses, as its field engineers travel by public transport or in the firm's minibus within the metropolitan area. This of course is also reflected in vehicle costs, which were 78% higher for E. Figure 10.3 shows a breakdown of costs for travel, expenses and vehicles.

E has generous travel allowances which were introduced about 10 years ago to compensate for relatively low salary levels. The company's low-pay image lived on as a myth; in fact the salaries it pays are fully comparable to their equivalents in other companies. The fact–based benchmarking approach gave the lie to this fallacy.

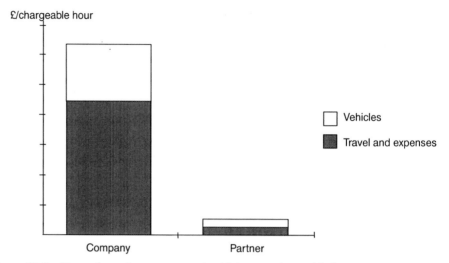

Figure 10.3   Costs of travel, expenses and vehicles per chargeable hour

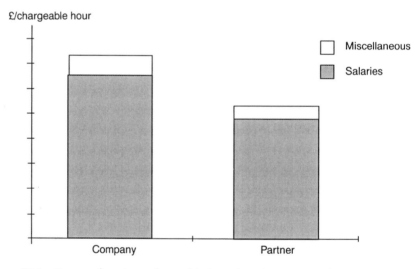

Figure 10.4   Personnel cost per chargeable hour for other personnel

In addition, E had a cost disadvantage of 30% compared to its partner in the 'other personnel' category, i.e. employees with staff-type duties and less than 50% chargeable time (Figure 10.4). A deliberate drive to reduce the size of the staff organization was initiated at once.

To sum up, the benchmarking exercise led to the following observations:

- E has a cost disadvantage of 18% per chargeable hour compared to its partner.
- To cope with increasing pressure of competition, E needs to do something about its

costs. The difference in personnel costs, for example, is so great that it is doubtful whether E can survive unless it scraps its present system of travel and expense allowances.

- Note that the partner, in addition to lower costs, also commands a broader range of skills.

Benchmarking recommendations and subsequent results

To meet future competition, E must get its costs closer to open-market levels. This calls for a thorough, critical review of all costs. E has a serious cost disadvantage relative to the best outside company with which it was compared.

Benchmarking led to the following changes:

- Review of existing terms of employment in consultation with personnel with a view to reducing travel and expense allowances.
- Abolition of hierarchical production management, with only one staff per department.
- Reduction of number of supervisory areas from one supervisor per 10 engineers to one per 25; no department to have more than 10 supervisory areas.
- Further functionalization of organization with more departmental specialization.
- Goals set for the new organization more closely related to external cost levels.

CASE 2

Background

This involves exploratory benchmarking of customer-perceived value in a manufacturing company. This case is included here to show that benchmarking can also be organized differently, and can be used to good effect with the emphasis on customer-perceived value.

ACE is a large engineering company of traditional type which sells its products and services worldwide. Its strong engineering tradition has prompted a focus on new sales of large pieces of machinery. Its culture is predominantly hi-tech-oriented, with complex designs featuring state-of-the-art technology as status symbols. Its explicit corporate mission was to be the technological leader in its field, and this influenced every part of its strategy and operations.

Aim of benchmarking

Benchmarking with broad focus on customer-perceived value

The company had fairly recently acquired a new management that wanted to base operations on more tangible facts about the two axes of the efficiency graph, i.e. value creation and productivity (see Chapter 1). Productivity was surveyed in a detailed study of relative cost position compared to a couple of other similar companies. That study revealed possibilities for substantial improvements in productivity, achieved mainly by changing the factory structure.

Now the management also wanted to acquire a fact base for the value variable, i.e. quality (utility) as a function of price.

Choice of benchmarking criteria

The first step was to determine customers' quality criteria. This was done by conducting a score of depth interviews in four countries. The criteria eventually chosen for assessment were:

- equipment features
- equipment reliability
- purchase price
- operating cost
- supplier's knowledge of customer's production
- delivery time of equipment
- precise product information
- easy to reach
- quick and precise answers to questions
- innovative suggestions for use of equipment in customer's business
- response time in field service
- price of technical service
- price of spare parts
- delivery time of spare parts
- geographical proximity to customer

Know your own organization

The various factors were not weighted in any particular way at this stage of the study.

The next step was to ask the parties concerned about the relative importance of each criterion. This was not done by the 'trade-off' method of asking them to choose between different criteria in order to get an appreciation of their relative importance; in this case the respondents were asked direct how much importance they attached to each criterion.

To get an idea of the degree of self-knowledge in the organization, the questions were put to three groups of respondents:

(1) Customers (about their own opinions);
(2) Employees of a national sales company (about their perceptions of customers' priorities);
(3) Employees at the head office (about their perceptions of customers' priorities).

The results of the poll are shown in Figure 10.5.

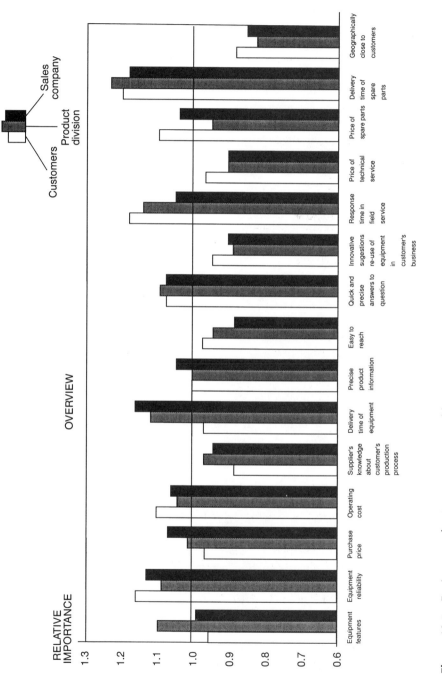

Figure 10.5 Equipment selection criteria as rated by customers, sales company and head office

The results of the poll led to a discussion about the degree of self-knowledge in the organization, in view of the following observations:

(1) The head office had greatly overrated the importance of advanced technical features, which customers did not in fact consider essential.

(2) The organization, especially the sales company, overrated the importance of price.

(3) The organization was also wrong about delivery time for new equipment. Customers were not at all as insistent on this as the ACE people assumed.

(4) Response time for field service was rated much higher by customers than by the organization itself.

(5) The prices of technical service and spare parts were also much more important to customers than ACE had believed.

Choice of benchmarking partners

When the customers had weighted each criterion, customers in no fewer than 22 countries were asked to assess ACE's performance compared to its chief competitor, whose name varied from one country to another; comparisons were made with different competitors in Japan, France, Australia and Canada for example. The results of this poll appear in Figure 10.6.

Results of the analysis

The bars in Figure 10.6 are the same as in Figure 10.5; they show customers' importance ratings of each factor. The points connected by lines indicate customers' judgements of ACE's performance in each respect, as compared to its chief competitor on their respective markets.

Some of the results confirmed previous management assessments, but some came as a total surprise:

(1) ACE was great at 'bells and whistles', i.e. technical refinements secondary to the principal function of the equipment. Customers, alas, did not rate this as very important.

(2) Reliability and operating costs were very important, but ACE was not given specially high scores on those points.

(3) Ratings of ACE's after-market performance came as a shock to the management. The questions about response times, spare part and service prices and spare part delivery times received very dusty answers.

The management already knew that technological leadership had more to do with organizational self-realization than customer demand, so that finding was no surprise to them.

What did surprise them when the material was presented was the dismal after-market performance ratings. The management took this as a loud and clear signal that the company needed to do better. It appeared that the after-market had been neglected in

Figure 10.6 Relative performance of ACE compared to its chief competitor(s)

favour of making new sales of large and complex equipment. Responsibility had not been controlled, despite the fact that the after-market was both profitable and important to sales of new equipment. The person responsible for the after-market turned out to be a young graduate engineer, aged 31. His reaction was: 'That's what I've been saying for years, but nobody listened!'

This relatively young man occupied a lowly place in the corporate pecking-order, and bore staff responsibility for a low-status function. After-market responsibility at sales company level had diffused to the point of 'collective irresponsibility'. One of the worst cases was in an important market where the accountant had been put in charge of spare parts. He had added mark-ups of several thousand per cent to the prices of trivial parts, which had greatly irritated the buyers.

Benchmarking recommendations and subsequent results

The conclusion, to sum up, was that ACE had failed to recognize the after-market for what it really was—an essential part of their total business. The study led to a reorganization in which the product sales management in each country was also made responsible for after-market sales.

After this exploratory exercise in benchmarking quality, ACE followed up with a comparative study of work processes in its sales companies. Organizations, systems, pricing, delivery routines, etc. were surveyed in detail, and lessons from the best performers were communicated to every function and process. This led, as far as the after-market was concerned, to a steady improvement of competitive position in the 22 countries where the study was conducted.

CASE 3

Background

This is a case of benchmarking of productivity in the retail trade. A cascade approach with two successive levels of resolution was used in this instance. The focus was on work processes.

A Telecom monopoly in a European country has a number of sidelines. One of them is a retail chain of about 200 Telecom shops whose primary function is to give the anonymous organization a living face to present to private subscribers and small firms.

The actual core business, with a turnover reckoned in billions of pounds, is divided among 22 districts, each with a district manager who enjoys considerable authority. The district managers wield such great power partly as a result of the Telecom operator's importance as a local employer.

Management of the 200 shops was characterized by a low degree of co-ordination and a high degree of influence from the monopoly operator's administrative systems.

Aim of benchmarking

The Telecom operator's central management desired to throw light on its retail business from the standpoint of productivity. They wanted to find external reference points (benchmarks) to be able to judge how far they could push rationalization without sacrificing the quality of service.

The aim of the project was to compile a fact base for decisions on a two-stage programme of development and efficiency enhancement in the retail chain:

Stage 1: Rationalizing the existing structure.
Stage 2: Finding out whether any structural action could be taken to take better advantage of specialization and economies of scale.

The project focused mainly on the productivity aspect in the shops; it did not encompass the matter of customer-perceived value.

The analysis was performed in two ways:

(1)   *Micro scale:* Each individual function was studied with a view to rationalization.
(2)   *Macro scale:* The whole operation was evaluated.

The results of both parts of the study agreed and were thus considered as verified.

Choice of benchmarking partners

The benchmarking partners were Chain X, which was in a comparable line of business (office equipment and supplies), and Chain Y, which was reckoned to be the best performer in the retail trade at large.

Chain X

Chain X recently scrapped its regional structure in favour of a central organization with a tightly controlled logistic system. It uses three separate sales and distribution channels: consumer sales, company sales (cash and carry) and door-to-door sales reps.

The focus in this study was on consumer sales, which most closely resembled the Telecom shop business.

Chain X broke even in the year the study was made.

Chain Y

Chain Y is seen as the national retail trade champion. It works with a very narrow overhead organization and a tightly controlled concept.

The shops are responsible for customer care, sales and personnel, while the head office handles product range, stock replenishment, pricing, marketing and shop location.

Chain Y is highly profitable.

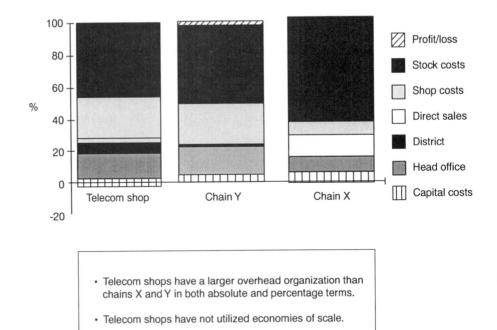

Figure 10.7   Total value chains as percentages of turnover

The Telecom shops had a matrix organization in which operative matters were handled at district level while strategic issues like product range, pricing and marketing were largely the responsibility of the head office. The latter also handled product development and export sales. Logistics and stockkeeping were purchased from other functions.

Each district had a local retail organization. Other resources were purchased from the district management, and the costs booked varied widely from one district to another.

Benchmarking study

The value chains of the organizations were stated both in absolute terms and as percentages. Figure 10.7 shows an example of the latter.

As our clients' overhead costs were much higher than their partners', we decided to analyse that aspect in more detail. Figure 10.8 shows these costs at a finer level of resolution.

Information gathering and analysis

One striking observation was that accounting principles were not the same. Cost distribution practice varied enormously between the 22 districts. This was also one of the reasons why surpluses varied so much.

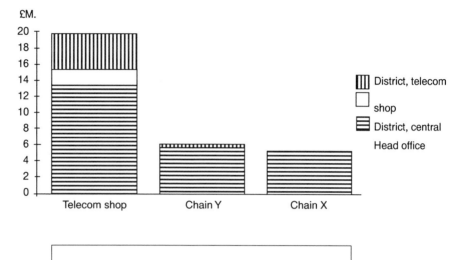

£M.

- District, telecom
- shop
- District, central
  Head office

- Telecom shops' overheads are twice as high.
- Telecom shops have not utilized economies of scale.

Figure 10.8   Total costs of overhead organization

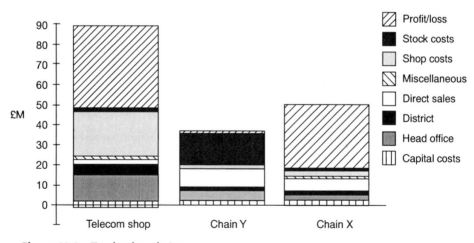

£M

Profit/loss
Stock costs
Shop costs
Miscellaneous
Direct sales
District
Head office
Capital costs

Figure 10.9   Total value chains

Figure 10.10 was drawn by measuring the number of customers relative to the number of staff in a shop. Customers were counted by wiring the door to signal every time it opened. The number of customers is shown divided by five simply to make the curves more easily comparable. It is evident that manning in the shop is not controlled by floor traffic; staff are at lunch during the hour when the number of customers is greatest. This graph really shocked the client.

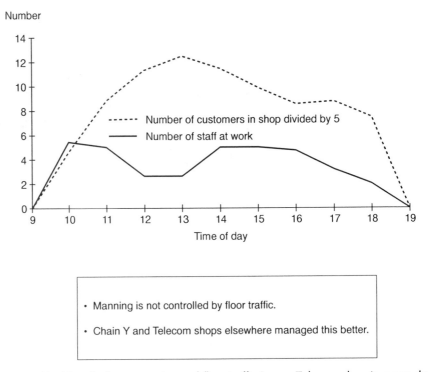

Number

Figure 10.10   Hour-by-hour manning and floor traffic in one Telecom shop (average day)

Analysis of operative content

The analysis shown in Figure 10.11 was made by asking shop staff how they spent their time. Staff in the six Telecom shops that were analysed in depth (A–F) spent relatively little time actually selling, while those in Chain Y shops spent nearly all their time selling. One of the Chain X shops was a cash–and–carry store with a sizeable proportion of logistic personnel.

The duties of Chain Y staff consist in keeping the shop clean and tidy and selling goods. Our client, the Telecom shops, employed well–educated staff and had by far the highest personnel costs.

Results of benchmarking

Figure 10.12 shows the split between full–time and part–time employees. It appears at first sight that the Telecom shops optimized manning handily with the help of part–time staff, but such was not in fact the case. Part–time working was determined not by the employer but by the employees, who might want to shorten their working hours in order to care for children, etc.

Chain Y, by contrast, operates on the principle of having only one full–time employee—the manager(ess)—per shop; all the others are part–timers.

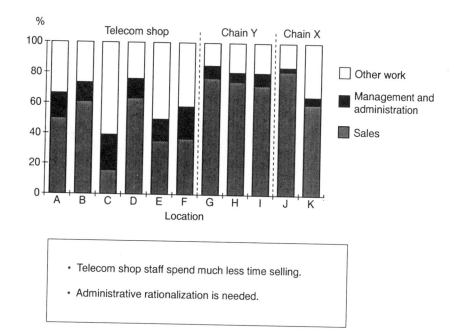

Figure 10.11   Analysis of how staff in shops spend their time

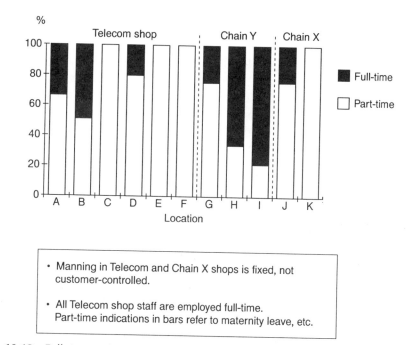

Figure 10.12   Full-time and part-time staff in shops

To assess the costs of shop premises, a real-estate consultant was engaged to evaluate floor space and how it was used in the six Telecom shops that were studied in detail. The findings were firstly that an unduly large proportion of the available space was used for purposes other than selling, and secondly that the rentals, often paid to the Telecom Group's own property management company, were higher than the going rate for shop premises in the areas concerned.

The client used all this information to initiate a large number of implementation projects focused on planning, logistics, space utilization, etc.

CASE 4

INTERNATIONAL BENCHMARKING

This is an example of exploratory benchmarking with a large number of partners to identify areas that merit analysis in depth together with one or more partners.

Background

Providing the inhabitants of a country with telecommunications services has been a government responsibility ever since the invention of the telephone. Governments have delegated this responsibility to a state-owned or private operator which normally held a monopoly in its own country. As a result, national operators have been able to collaborate, compare data and pool experience, because they were not in competition with each other.

One problem with such comparisons was that the organizations concerned were not analysed in depth, and the units of measurement used were not consistently defined.

Now that the world of telecommunications is exposed to competition and owners (usually governments) are demanding higher revenues, telecom operators are being forced to do something about their profitability. Yet they cannot do so by putting up their prices, which are controlled by the same governments.

Their only option, then, is to improve productivity—to produce more at lower cost. They can do this for example by doing the same work with fewer people, getting the same number of people to do more work, or reducing their peripheral costs.

One European telecom operator, ETO 3, had already dismissed 15% of its workforce, so there were no more savings to be made by that route. At the same time the management was unsure of where further cost reductions could be made in the organization, and how.

ETO 3 decided to conduct an exploratory benchmarking project with several American telecom operators and a few in Europe. The latter were chosen on grounds of access to information and willingness, time and resources to participate in the project.

Aim of benchmarking

What to benchmark

The first step was to decide what to benchmark. This was done with reference to ETO 3's operations and the American operators' ability to provide information. The aim of the definition was to find a model that would both reflect the basics of telecom operation and offer a high degree of comparability. This meant cutting out all sidelines, for example.

However, it was finally decided to treat certain types of telecom-related business as bought-in services. Thus computer service costs were included, but not computer department personnel.

The functions subjected to benchmarking were:

- planning and project engineering
- construction
- operation and maintenance
- marketing and sales

The next problem was how to handle differences in organizational structure. One partner was extremely decentralized, while others had more centralized structures, and this was also reflected in accounting practices. Personnel job descriptions, however, proved more manageable, so these were used as a basis for cost distribution.

Comparability

As previously noted, the members of the industry to which this study referred had a historical tradition of comparing themselves to each other. Their business operations, however, had not been rigorously defined, with the result that the comparisons had been severely criticized. In addition, there are many who maintain that comparisons are pointless because a telecom service operating in a thinly populated region is not comparable to one in a metropolitan area.

The factors judged to affect comparability were therefore normalized.

Figure 10.13 illustrates how the results of regression analysis can be presented. Four parameters had been picked out as non-comparable factors. One of them was geographical coverage, illustrated in the lower left-hand graph.

The next step in the regression analysis was to combine these four factors into an overall adjustment factor. Most of the adjustments were found to lie within a range of $\pm 10\%$, though three extreme cases of up to 25% adjustment were also noted.

Finally, personnel costs were also adjusted to ETO 3's level. This is an important point to bear in mind in an international comparison.

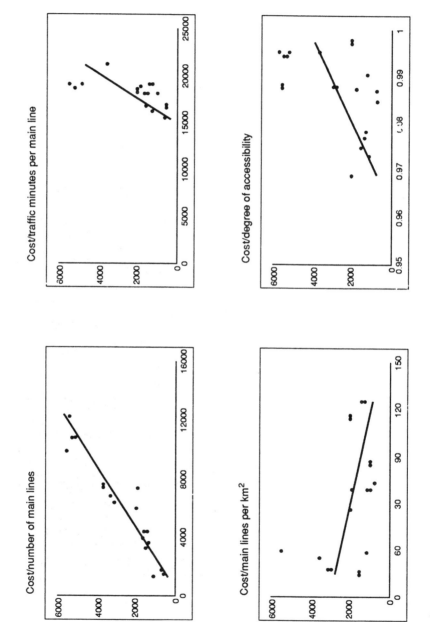

Figure 10.13 Regression analysis of costs

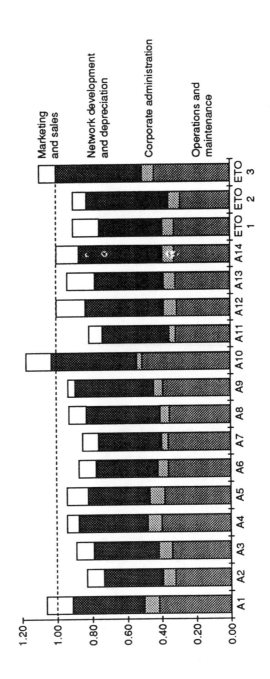

Figure 10.14 Network services: total normalized costs broken down by functions

Results of low-resolution exploratory benchmarking

At the time of the exercise, ETO 3's cost-efficiency was 7% below average, calculated on normalized figures (Figure 10.14). ETO 3's productivity was more than 20% below that of the best operator in the study.

ETO 3 was now faced with the crucial question of which areas to choose for the focus of further benchmarking.

Analysis of costs per function showed that the greatest potential existed in the area of network operation and maintenance.

At the same time a closer analysis of planning and project engineering costs revealed that ETO 3's R&D costs were about four times higher than its partners'. One reason for this was that ETO 3's purchasing policies had historically differed from those of its partners, with the result that it had only one supplier of certain critical products, and had to bear a large share of that supplier's development costs.

ETO 3 decided to invite two partners to collaborate on a deeper benchmarking exercise. One of them was European, and the other American.

Availability at the time, together with the fact that the American operator was then working hard at rationalizing its non-personnel costs, decided the choice of partners. The European partner, moreover, was differently organized and used subcontractors to a greater extent than ETO 3 did.

In-depth benchmarking of selected areas

Operation and maintenance

The deeper analysis showed even more clearly that ETO 3 was inefficient in the area of other costs; it used twice as much office space as its partners, for example. In addition, it had five to seven times as many technical buildings, which imposed a further cost burden on its operations.

ETO 3 had also, unlike its partners, entrusted the management of its properties to a real-estate firm. The resulting rental contracts were disadvantageous to ETO 3, while the real-estate firm earned a handsome profit. Rentals for technical buildings, which could not be used for any other purpose, had been set at the going market rate, whereas ETO 3's partners had written off their technical buildings entirely. Does this not distort the analysis? No, for the comparison reflects the costs that the businesses had to bear.

A further problem for ETO 3 was that the large number of technical stations not only cost more in rentals but were also more expensive to operate and maintain and had a high fault frequency.

ETO 3 also had purely organizational opportunities to improve its operation and maintenance productivity. The American partner had done a great deal of process mapping in this area and had drawn up guidelines for how local work was to be done. At ETO, by contrast, it took about 20 work processes to achieve the same result.

It was further found that ETO 3 lagged somewhat behind its partners in updating its technology, which also affected its ability to operate and maintain its facilities productively.

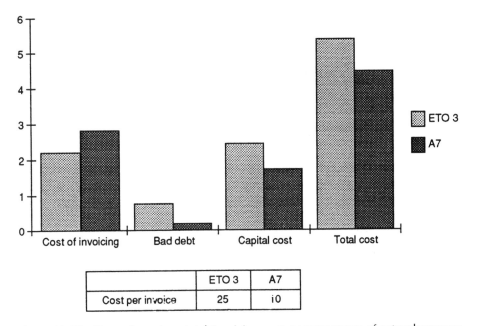

	ETO 3	A7
Cost per invoice	25	i0

Figure 10.15   Network services: total invoicing costs as percentages of network revenue

In return, ETO 3 was able to furnish its partners with information about trouble-shooting; the analysis had shown that ETO 3 was highly successful in this respect.

Finally, an analysis was also made of invoicing routines. In this case ETO 3 turned out to be more productive than its partners, especially the American one, in terms of normalized total costs. The American partner, however, got more out of its invoicing because it billed its customers monthly; naturally, this influenced interest costs and bad debts (Figure 10.15).

Results of benchmarking

- ETO 3's operative profit centres have been allowed to get rid of premises that they do not need; this has been a great encouragement to further rationalization.
- Purchasing policy has been changed; ETO 3 is now required always to have at least two suppliers.
- Process management of operations and maintenance has been introduced; the aim is to establish uniform processes within ETO 3.
- To boost productivity in invoicing, process management and design of comprehensive computerized support systems have been initiated.

This phase of benchmarking has enabled various units of the ETO 3 organization to relinquish premises that are surplus to requirements—an encouraging step on the road to cost saving and rationalization.

11
Follow-up and benchlearning

It is important that a successful benchmarking process is followed up and that proposed improvements are actually implemented. The whole point of a benchmarking exercise is to achieve the envisioned improvement and be able to measure it by a subsequent study.

UNIVERSAL INVOLVEMENT

A well-run benchmarking process generates a strong sense of involvement on the part of all concerned. Everybody takes a keen interest in the proposed improvements, which are seen as an integral part of the job. We can capture this interest and utilize it to create a desire for continual improvement of the organization. The enthusiasm of the participants becomes a powerful efficiency-boosting tool in itself.

SKILL DEVELOPMENT AS A TOOL FOR EFFICIENCY

The question that all chief executives and managers will be required to answer in the 1990s is: 'How efficient is your business?' (Efficiency is the product of customer utility and productivity.) To be able to answer that question they will need a good, fact-based analytical instrument, and to demonstrate a satisfactory level of efficiency they will need access to a number of efficiency-boosting tools.

Two routes to efficiency

Benchmarking is a proven method of measuring the efficiency of a business. A properly performed benchmarking analysis can point to areas of potential improvement and focus on action that will make operations more efficient. This may involve both action to enhance customer utility and action to increase productivity.

Various forms of rationalization have been practised in the recent recession. Companies that have still not fully rationalized their operations may find it hard to keep up with the field when the market starts growing again, for their relative productivity may be too low. At the same time, companies that have still not focused their attention on customer utility will be in trouble when market demands grow more insistent.

The third way

A third way to be more efficient is to use internal resources more creatively, i.e. to develop the skills of your people within the framework of the business.

NEW ROUTES TO EFFICIENCY

The demands of the 1990s will call for new ways of improving efficiency. The most successful way may be to utilize skill development as a tool of efficiency. A new view of skill development, together with previous experience, can be the new route to efficiency.

Rationalization has taken different forms in different decades, all the way from the MTM (Measure Time Method) to *Kaizen* (Japanese management term for continuous step by step improvement). In the 1980s the focus was on customers and quality. How many training courses have there been with titles like 'The Customer in the Centre' or 'Right from the Start'? At various times we have taught our managers the leadership doctrines of one prophet or another. Occasionally we have even taught our employees how to be nice to each other.

Efficiency in training

It is hard to tell how effective these teaching efforts have been. We believe on general principle that all skill development is good for an organization, but the effect varies, and not all methods are equally cost-effective. Let us go back to the question in the first paragraph: 'How efficient is your business?'. Can you measure the efficiency of training? Yes, of course you can. Not by asking the participants whether they were satisfied with the food, the hotel or the instructor, but by measuring the effect on day-to-day business. Skill development must be goal-oriented, and the goal must be to guide the business in some direction. Many training activities, unfortunately, have aimed at imparting a specified amount of knowledge rather than at increasing the profits of the business by X pounds or marks or francs. It is difficult to measure the value of increasing knowledge in relation to the cost that the company incurs thereby. But it is easy to measure actual results in relation to actual costs.

FACT-BASED SKILL DEVELOPMENT

Favourable experience of benchmarking confirms that fact-based analyses are a good form of input for skill development. By deciding in advance what areas need skill development the most, we can make fact-based measurements of effect both before and after.

In all the benchmarking assignments that the authors have undertaken over the years, we have been impressed by the enthusiasm of the participants. The act of compiling a fact base about a business makes it easy to motivate changes. Interest on the part of those who assemble and analyse the facts is keen, and their will to go further often generates a strong need for skill development.

Fact-based skill development

This in turn has given rise to a new kind of fact-based skill development which we call *benchlearning*. The important thing about *benchlearning* is not so much that it represents a new view of skill development, but that it is a powerful aid to efficiency.

Benchlearning is the third way to make your business more efficient, by leadership development combined with total involvement on the part of all employees.

BENCHLEARNING

On-the-job learning

The essence of benchlearning is that participants work the whole time at their own jobs, and learn to make the organization's operations more efficient through skill development derived from fact-based analyses. They acquire an ability to solve problems combined with an eagerness to learn that lays the foundations for continual improvement. The proven value of training facilitates the transition from thought to action. Theory is combined with practice, and skill development becomes an integral part of efficiency improvement.

Foundation

The foundation of benchlearning is a method of fact-based analysis which leads to:

- concrete action
- traditional formal education
- on-the-job training and mentorship
- motivation programmes for all employees
- more fact-based analysis

This last step is preceded by a stocktaking of skills, which in turn is based on a general discussion of goals with various parts of the business.

Integrating all skill development schemes into the mainstream of the business creates a natural climate of change and a *learning organization*. A further result of this integration is that skill development is acquired at no extra cost. These are in any event matters which should occupy the attention of managers, but the benchlearning programme helps them to rank strategic questions in order of importance as well as to improve precision in operative matters. That is the foundation of successful leadership—a difficult art.

12
Work forms

Table 12.1 Plan of action

Activity	Purpose	Person in charge	Timetable	Goal

Table 12.2 Benchmarking planning checklist

Decide what to benchmark	Has our own business been mapped out? Have our own processes been identified? Have the customers and suppliers of these processes been identified? Has the level of detail for benchmarking been decided?
Identify benchmarking partners	Decide upon type of partner Search for partners Identify the partner's main processes Secure acceptance of participation
Gather information	Has the type of information needed been clearly defined? Is information from our organization readily available? Is information available from outside sources? Have we compiled explanatory information? Is the quality of the information controlled? Have we checked the information against our needs? Correct for non-comparable factors
Analyse	Has the information been correctly compiled? Can a gap in performance be observed? Can factors that explain the gap be found?
Implement	Has the result of the benchmarking study been accepted by the organization? Can the results be integrated with our regular business plan? Have alterations of main processes been identified? Have enough resources been allocated to implementation of the changes? Have our skills improved?

Table 12.3 Business process/function matrix

Main processes and subprocesses	Functions					
	Sales	Production	Development	Marketing	Finance	Logistics
Customer orders						
Customer relations						
Pricing						
Production						
Distribution						
Packing						
Purchasing						
Supplier relations						
Development						
Prototypes						
Market research						
After-market						
Customer complaints						
Field service						
Guarantees						
Business control						
Budgeting						
Financing						
Recruitment						
Personnel development						
Strategic planning						

Evaluation of strength: ■ Strong ▓ Average ▒ Weak

Table 12.4   Benchmarking process description

Description of process (diagram)	
Functions to which process belongs and handovers between separate functions	
Objectives of process	
Customers for process	
Suppliers to process	

Targets for process performance			
	Present level	Trend	Target
Costs			
Time			
Quality measurements			

Table 12.5   Benchmarking process questionnaire

(1)   Describe the process, its purpose, its objectives and the functions involved, with special emphasis on cross-overs between functions.

(2)   How does this process influence the company's goals and 'its earnings?

(3)   How can this process be measured in terms of cost, quality and time? How would you define a high standard in these terms? How can improvements be measured?

(4)   What categories of personnel are involved in this process, and what types of skills are needed?

(5)   The process does not perform as it should, or costs too much. Has it ever been reconstructed before, and if so how?

(6)   What conceivable benchmarking partners exist?

Table 12.6   Determination of benchmarking criteria (BC)

Benchmarked process(es)	
Proposed measurements	
Reason for choice of measurements	
'Owner' of process	

Key questions
(1)   Do the BC give a thorough and relevant description of the process?
(2)   The number of BC used should be kept as small as possible. Can certain criteria be omitted?
(3)   Can relevant data be obtained?
(4)   What data are quantifiable/not quantifiable?
(5)   Can the BC be measured over a period of time?
(6)   Are the BC recognized internally/externally?
(7)   Does an improvement in the BC mean that the whole process is improved?
(8)   How would a radical improvement in the BC affect the company's net income?

Table 12.7   Business comparison: key indicator analysis

Indicators		Company		
		X	Y	Z
Return on equity after tax income	%			
Return on working capital before tax	%			
Solidity				
Capital turnover rate				
Inventory				
Balance sheet total				
Sales per employee	$			
R&D costs	% of sales			
Return on investments				
Net financial result	% of sales			
Warranty costs	%			
Market share	%			
Goods returned	% of deliveries			

Table 12.8   Benchmarking partner analysis

Characteristics		Companies		
Size	Sales			
	No. of employees			
Ownership	Public companies: 5 largest shareholders			
	Closely held companies: families			
Business concept/mission				
Main products				
Organization	Functional			
	Divisionalized			
	Matrix			
	Other			
Cultural factors	Formalism			
	Group control			
	Openness			
Specific business skills				
Strategy				

Table 12.9 Benchmarking: new goals

Critical success parameters	Measures of performance			Partner
Process	Present level	Short-term goal Year	Long-term goal Year	Company: Date:

Changes needed to attain goals
Short-term:
Long-term:

Table 12.10   Benchmarking implementation plan

	Company			
	Own company	Partner X	Partner Y	Partner Z
Benchmarked process:				
Process owner:				
Measures of performance:				
Goals				
Short-term:				
Long-term:				
Describe desired result:				

Table 12.11   Project description

Name of project:
Person in charge:
Members of project group:

Purpose of project:

Description of project:

Requirements for implementation/investments:

Consequences:

Timetable/allocation of responsibilities:

Table 12.12 Determination of customer-perceived value

| Product group: .... |
| Customer category: Internal .... External .... |

Selection criteria	Supplier How do we think the customer will rate utility factors?					Supplier How do we rate importance?					Customer What is the contractor's delivery capability?				
	Most important 5	4	3	Not important 2	1	Most important 5	4	3	Not important 2	1	Good 5	4	3	2	Bad 1
Low price															
Delivery on schedule															
Accessible for enquiries															
Takes full responsibility															
Uses new technology															
High technical quality and competence															
Uses proven technology															
Easy to buy from															
Understands what customers want															
Flexible and quick															
Known contact person															
Provides customer training															
Takes account of future requirements															
Courteous and helpful															
Specified invoices															
Gives guarantees															
ISO 9000 certified															
Right first time															
Can give references															
Environment conscious															

Table 12.13   Benchmarking: shop questionnaire (1994 results)

| Region .... | | Shop .... | |

	Product	Services	Miscellaneous	Total
Sales External	[_____]	[_____]	[_____]	[_____]
Internal	[_____]	[_____]	[_____]	[_____]
Commissions	[_____]	[_____]	[_____]	[_____]
Margin contribution 1	[_____]	[_____]	[_____]	[_____]
Margin contribution 1%	[_____]	[_____]	[_____]	[_____]
Price reductions %	[_____]	[_____]	[_____]	[_____]
Wastage %	[_____]	[_____]	[_____]	[_____]
Discounts %	[_____]	[_____]	[_____]	[_____]
Direct costs:				
Personnel	[_____]	[_____]	[_____]	[_____]
Premises, total	[_____]	[_____]	[_____]	[_____]
Marketing, national	[_____]	[_____]	[_____]	[_____]
Marketing, local	[_____]	[_____]	[_____]	[_____]
Computer system	[_____]	[_____]	[_____]	[_____]
Training	[_____]	[_____]	[_____]	[_____]
Miscellaneous	[_____]	[_____]	[_____]	[_____]
Depreciation	[_____]	[_____]	[_____]	[_____]
Indirect costs:				
Region	[_____]	[_____]	[_____]	[_____]
Retail organization	[_____]	[_____]	[_____]	[_____]
Inventory booked 31/12	[_____]	[_____]	[_____]	[_____]
Shop area, m^2	[_____]	[_____]	[_____]	[_____]
of which sales area, m^2	[_____]	[_____]	[_____]	[_____]
Employees:				
on 1 Jan 1994	[_____]	[_____]	[_____]	[_____]
on 31 Dec 1994	[_____]	[_____]	[_____]	[_____]
Average for year	[_____]	[_____]	[_____]	[_____]
Directly connected to Head Office	[___] Yes	[___] No		
Catchment area (population)	[_____]			
Location:	[_____]			

(Well or badly situated urban, shopping centre, rural)

Table 12.14 Benchmarking: personnel analysis

					Total	Remarks
MARKET	**Market**	. . . .	. . . .	. . . .	. . . .	
	Market analysis	. . . .	. . . .	. . . .	. . . .	
	Market planning	. . . .	. . . .	. . . .	. . . .	
	Other (. . . . .)	. . . .	. . . .	. . . .	. . . .	
	Advertising					
	Marketing communications	. . . .	. . . .	. . . .	. . . .	
	Artwork	. . . .	. . . .	. . . .	. . . .	
	Sales promotion	. . . .	. . . .	. . . .	. . . .	
	Point-of-sale material	. . . .	. . . .	. . . .	. . . .	
	Other (. . . . .)	. . . .	. . . .	. . . .	. . . .	
PRODUCT	**Product specification**	. . . .	. . . .	. . . .	. . . .	
	Product knowledge	. . . .	. . . .	. . . .	. . . .	
	Product range composition	. . . .	. . . .	. . . .	. . . .	
	Product range strategy	. . . .	. . . .	. . . .	. . . .	
	Sales planning	. . . .	. . . .	. . . .	. . . .	
	Other (. . . . .)	. . . .	. . . .	. . . .	. . . .	
PRODUCT DEVELOPMENT	**Product development**	. . . .	. . . .	. . . .	. . . .	
	Idea	. . . .	. . . .	. . . .	. . . .	
	Specification	. . . .	. . . .	. . . .	. . . .	
	Development	. . . .	. . . .	. . . .	. . . .	
	Testing	. . . .	. . . .	. . . .	. . . .	
	Documentation	. . . .	. . . .	. . . .	. . . .	
	Other (. . . . .)	. . . .	. . . .	. . . .	. . . .	
PURCHASING	**Purchasing**	. . . .	. . . .	. . . .	. . . .	
	Contact with suppliers	. . . .	. . . .	. . . .	. . . .	
	Cost negotiations	. . . .	. . . .	. . . .	. . . .	
	Other (. . . . .)	. . . .	. . . .	. . . .	. . . .	
	Ordering	. . . .	. . . .	. . . .	. . . .	
	Piecemeal buying	. . . .	. . . .	. . . .	. . . .	
	Other (. . . . .)	. . . .	. . . .	. . . .	. . . .	
LOGISTICS	**Dispatching**	. . . .	. . . .	. . . .	. . . .	
	Shipping	. . . .	. . . .	. . . .	. . . .	
	Other (. . . . .)	. . . .	. . . .	. . . .	. . . .	
	Stocks	. . . .	. . . .	. . . .	. . . .	
	Storeroom work	. . . .	. . . .	. . . .	. . . .	
	Picking	. . . .	. . . .	. . . .	. . . .	
	Reception	. . . .	. . . .	. . . .	. . . .	
	Stocktaking	. . . .	. . . .	. . . .	. . . .	
	Data input	. . . .	. . . .	. . . .	. . . .	
	Other (. . . . .)	. . . .	. . . .	. . . .	. . . .	
ADMINISTRATION	**Personnel**	. . . .	. . . .	. . . .	. . . .	
	Salaries and wages	. . . .	. . . .	. . . .	. . . .	
	Union agreements	. . . .	. . . .	. . . .	. . . .	
	Consultation	. . . .	. . . .	. . . .	. . . .	
	Training	. . . .	. . . .	. . . .	. . . .	
	Other (. . . . .)	. . . .	. . . .	. . . .	. . . .	
	Accounting	. . . .	. . . .	. . . .	. . . .	
	Ledger	. . . .	. . . .	. . . .	. . . .	
	Customer and supplier accounts	. . . .	. . . .	. . . .	. . . .	
	Invoicing	. . . .	. . . .	. . . .	. . . .	
	Payments	. . . .	. . . .	. . . .	. . . .	
	Budgeting	. . . .	. . . .	. . . .	. . . .	
	Costing	. . . .	. . . .	. . . .	. . . .	
	Other (. . . . .)	. . . .	. . . .	. . . .	. . . .	

					Total	Remarks
ADMINISTRATION	**Quality**	. . . .	. . . .	. . . .	. . . .	
(continued)	Follow-up of ISO 9000	. . . .	. . . .	. . . .	. . . .	
	Standardization	. . . .	. . . .	. . . .	. . . .	
	Other (. . . . .)	. . . .	. . . .	. . . .	. . . .	
	Internal service	. . . .	. . . .	. . . .	. . . .	
	Building	. . . .	. . . .	. . . .	. . . .	
	Office	. . . .	. . . .	. . . .	. . . .	
	Cleaning	. . . .	. . . .	. . . .	. . . .	
	Delivery	. . . .	. . . .	. . . .	. . . .	
	PABX	. . . .	. . . .	. . . .	. . . .	
	Other (. . . . .)	. . . .	. . . .	. . . .	. . . .	
	Secretarial	. . . .	. . . .	. . . .	. . . .	
	Typing	. . . .	. . . .	. . . .	. . . .	
	Bookings	. . . .	. . . .	. . . .	. . . .	
	Other (. . . . .)	. . . .	. . . .	. . . .	. . . .	
SALES	**Cash register**	. . . .	. . . .	. . . .	. . . .	
	Behind counter in shop	. . . .	. . . .	. . . .	. . . .	
	Other (. . . . .)	. . . .	. . . .	. . . .	. . . .	
	Customer contact	. . . .	. . . .	. . . .	. . . .	
	Telephone	. . . .	. . . .	. . . .	. . . .	
	In shop	. . . .	. . . .	. . . .	. . . .	
	Sale of services	. . . .	. . . .	. . . .	. . . .	
	Sale of products	. . . .	. . . .	. . . .	. . . .	
	Other sales	. . . .	. . . .	. . . .	. . . .	
	Enquiries	. . . .	. . . .	. . . .	. . . .	
	Other (. . . . .)	. . . .	. . . .	. . . .	. . . .	
	Other sales work	. . . .	. . . .	. . . .	. . . .	
	Outdoor selling	. . . .	. . . .	. . . .	. . . .	
	Other (. . . . .)	. . . .	. . . .	. . . .	. . . .	
MANAGEMENT	**Management**	. . . .	. . . .	. . . .	. . . .	
	Costing	. . . .	. . . .	. . . .	. . . .	
	Monitoring and control	. . . .	. . . .	. . . .	. . . .	
	Other (. . . . .)	. . . .	. . . .	. . . .	. . . .	
AFTER-MARKET	**Servicing**	. . . .	. . . .	. . . .	. . . .	
	Repairs	. . . .	. . . .	. . . .	. . . .	
	Maintenance	. . . .	. . . .	. . . .	. . . .	
	Other (. . . . .)	. . . .	. . . .	. . . .	. . . .	
DATA	**EDP system**	. . . .	. . . .	. . . .	. . . .	
PROCESSING	Development	. . . .	. . . .	. . . .	. . . .	
	Salaries and wages	. . . .	. . . .	. . . .	. . . .	
	Sales	. . . .	. . . .	. . . .	. . . .	
	Logistics	. . . .	. . . .	. . . .	. . . .	
	Operations	. . . .	. . . .	. . . .	. . . .	
	Miscellaneous	. . . .	. . . .	. . . .	. . . .	
	Other (. . . . .)	. . . .	. . . .	. . . .	. . . .	

Make a separate list here of services bought in from region or elsewhere:

. . . .	. . . .	. . . .	. . . .
. . . .	. . . .	. . . .	. . . .
. . . .	. . . .	. . . .	. . . .
. . . .	. . . .	. . . .	. . . .
. . . .	. . . .	. . . .	. . . .
. . . .	. . . .	. . . .	. . . .
. . . .	. . . .	. . . .	. . . .
. . . .	. . . .	. . . .	. . . .

Table 12.15   Data acquisition form—sales efficiency

| Salesperson | | Week no. | |

| District | Customers | | Number |

Number of	Cold calls	Telephone	_____	Number
		Personal	_____	Number
	Meetings	New customers	_____	Number
		Old customers	_____	Number
	Quotations		_____	Number
	Contacts	New customers	_____	Number
		Old customers	_____	Number

Customers per sales step		Suspects	_____	Number
		Prospects	_____	Number
		Ordering	_____	Number

Orders	Average order	Products	_____	£
		Accessories	_____	£
		Service agreement	_____	£
		Total	_____	£
	Number			Number
	Sales to New customers	_____	£	

Use of time	Cold calls	Telephone	————————	Hours
		Personal	————————	Hours
	Meetings	New customers	————————	Hours
		Old customers	————————	Hours
	Contacts	New customers	————————	Hours
		Old customers	————————	Hours
	Administration	Engineering	————————	Hours
		Quotations	————————	Hours
		Orders	————————	Hours
		Miscellaneous	————————	Hours
	Education	External	————————	Hours
		Internal	————————	Hours
	Training	External	————————	Hours
		Internal	————————	Hours
	Travel		————————	Hours
	Support of other functions	Service	————————	Hours
		Delivery	————————	Hours
	Other		————————	Hours

Company	Contact	Meeting

Table 12.16   Benchmarking

Region. . . . . Shop. . . . . Week no. . . . .

Monday

Time	Callers entering shop	Callers in shop known	unknown	Number of staff at work	Total transactions/ receipts
8–9					
9–10					
10–11					
11–12					
12–13					
13–14					
14–15					
15–16					
17–18					
18–19					

Sales   Product . . . .

Total . . . .

of which cash . . . .

of which invoiced . . . .

Table 12.16   (continued)

Region. . . . . Shop. . . . . Week no. . . . .

Tuesday

Time	Callers entering shop	Callers in shop		Number of staff at work	Total transactions/ receipts
		known	unknown		
8–9					
9–10					
10–11					
11–12					
12–13					
13–14					
14–15					
15–16					
17–18					
18–19					

Sales   Product . . . .

Total . . . .

of which cash . . . .

of which invoiced . . . .

Table 12.16   (continued)

Region. Shop. . . . . Week no. . . . .

Wednesday

Time	Callers entering shop	Callers in shop known	unknown	Number of staff at work	Total transactions/ receipts
8–9					
9–10					
10–11					
11–12					
12–13					
13–14					
14–15					
15–16					
17–18					
18–19					

Sales   Product. . . . .

             Total. . . . .

                of which cash. . . . .

                of which invoiced. . . . .

Table 12.16 (continued)

Region. Shop. . . . . Week no. . . . .

Thursday

Time	Callers entering shop	Callers in shop		Number of staff at work	Total transactions/ receipts
		known	unknown		
8–9					
9–10					
10–11					
11–12					
12–13					
13–14					
14–15					
15–16					
17–18					
18–19					

Sales   Product . . . .

                 Total . . . .

                       of which cash . . . .

                       of which invoiced . . . .

Table 12.16   (continued)

Region. . . . . of Shop. . . . . Week no. . . . .

Friday

Time	Callers entering shop	Callers in shop known	unknown	Number of staff at work	Total transactions/ receipts
8–9					
9–10					
10–11					
11–12					
12–13					
13–14					
14–15					
15–16					
17–18					
18–19					

Sales

Product . . . .

Total . . . .

of which cash . . . .

of which invoiced . . . .

Table 12.16   (continued)

Region. Shop. . . . . Week no. . . . .

Saturday

Time	Callers entering shop	Callers in shop known	unknown	Number of staff at work	Total transactions/ receipts
8–9					
9–10					
10–11					
11–12					
12–13					
13–14					
14–15					
15–16					
17–18					
18–19					

Sales   Product . . . .

                Total . . . .

                     of which cash . . . .

                     of which invoiced . . . .

Table 12.17   Benchmarking: personnel analysis
Date
Manager

List all employees, including those not at work (maternity leave, long illness, etc.)

Region

Shop

Name	Age	Education	Employed by company	Union member	Shop experience elsewhere Where?	Years	Time in shop	Salary

THE QUALITY
SYSTEMS MANUAL

The Definitive Guide to the ISO9000
Family and TickIT

TERENCE J. HALL

The Quality Systems Manual is relevant for every industry, whether manufacturing or service and provides hands-on information for Quality Managers, and those assigned to implement and maintain this new standard.

- A practical guide to the installation and maintenance of an ISO 9001 Quality System within a company, laid out to follow the exact format of the 20 clauses of ISO9001.

- Explains in plain English exactly how these causes should be applied to your business .

- Examines in detail TickIT the equivalent standard for 'software development' and shows how this integrates with ISO9001

- Designed as a practical guide to enable companies to register, the manual includes a section **Preparing for Assessment** to help optimise the chance of success when being formally assessed.

A third of the cost a company incurs in achieving registration is spent on consultant's fees. The cover price of this definitive guide would only buy you an hour of a consultant's time

Publication July 1995   0471 95588 4   £50.00   Paperback

(price correct at time of going to press but subject to change, please contact the New York office for prices in the USA)

Available from your bookseller or direct from the publisher

JOHN WILEY & SONS LTD, BAFFINS LANE, CHICHESTER, SUSSEX, PO19 1UD, UK
Tel: (+)1243 779777 Fax: (+)1243 775878

JOHN WILEY & SONS INC, 605 THIRD AVENUE, NEW YORK NY 10158-0012, USA
Tel: (212) 850 6000 Fax: (212) 850 6088